OSCAR W. McCONKIE

Jack

AARONIC PRIESTHOOD

Deseret Book Company
Salt Lake City, Utah
1977

© 1977 by Deseret Book Co.
All rights reserved
ISBN 0-87747-631-4
Printed in the United States of America

Library of Congress Cataloging in Publication Data
McConkie, Oscar Walter.
  Aaronic priesthood.

  Bibliography: p.
  Includes index.
  1. Aaronic Priesthood (Mormonism) I. Title.
BX 8659.5.M3   262'.09'3   77.3609
ISBN 0-87747-631-4

Contents

Preface

Several years ago I was commissioned by the Presiding Bishop of The Church of Jesus Christ of Latter-day Saints to write three manuals to be used as courses of study for those who bear the Aaronic Priesthood. These texts were *The Kingdom of God, God and Man,* and *The Priest in the Aaronic Priesthood.*

These books subsequently were translated into thirteen languages and distributed worldwide, and were the source material for teaching priests in the Aaronic Priesthood for three years. Several hundreds of thousands of copies were printed.

For some years these books have been out of print, and so this book, *Aaronic Priesthood,* draws from the previous works and brings together under one cover much of the research and information concerning the preparatory priesthood.

There is a need for such a book, I feel, for those who are called to bear this holy order as well as bishops and others assigned to stewardships in the order of Aaron. Parents whose sons bear the Aaronic Priesthood also need assistance in their responsibilities in rearing and giving instruction.

In this dispensation young men and boys are privileged to be called, as was Aaron, and ordained to the holy priesthood that bears his name. In order to magnify their callings they must understand what priesthood is and particularly, what the Aaronic Priesthood is. They must also understand its blessings and its concomitant responsibilities.

In this work I have attempted to give structure to the doctrines associated with the lesser or Aaronic Priesthood. I hope thus to enable those called to his holy order to utilize it as a "school master unto Christ," that is, a means by which to bring members of the Church and others to a fulness of the gospel. For thus was it given by the God of heaven to man on earth.

Acknowledgments

Special thanks is given to my brother, Bruce R. McConkie, for his careful reading of this text and the several suggestions he made. Appreciation is expressed also to my cousin, Merle D. Bryner, for typing the manuscript and for her valued opinions.

CHAPTER ONE

Priesthood and the Power of Righteousness

God has all power. There is no power that he does not possess. The risen Lord bore this testimony of his own omnipotence: "All power is given unto me in heaven and in earth." (Matthew 28:18.)

In this dispensation, the word of God has been heard through the voice of the Prophet Joseph Smith, saying, "Behold, and hearken unto the voice of him who has all power...." (D&C 61:1.) In the Book of Mormon the prophet Alma says that "we must come forth ... and acknowledge ... that he has all power." (Alma 12:15.) No truth about God is more fully witnessed in the holy scriptures than this. (See, for example, D&C 19:3, 4, 20; 20:24; 61:1; 93:17; 1 Nephi 9:6; Mormon 5:23; Ether 3:4.) John the Revelator seemed to hear the very elements proclaim, "Alleluia: for the Lord God omnipotent reigneth." (Revelation 19:6.) The word *omnipotent*, defined as having unlimited power and authority, is nearly always used as an adjective qualifying the noun *God*. (Joseph Smith, *Lectures on Faith*, pp. 9, 43-45, 50-51.)

One of the most gracious and loving doctrines taught by Jesus was the concept that man may share his power and authority. The Lord tells us that he will delegate this power and authority to man on earth to act in all things for the salvation of men. Indeed, Jesus specifically says he will empower those who believe on him to do the works that he did during his earthly ministry:

He that believeth on me, the works that I do shall he do also; and greater works than these shall he do; because I go unto my Father.

And whatsoever ye shall ask in my name, that will I do, that the Father may be glorified in the Son.

If ye shall ask any thing in my name, I will do it. (John 14:9, 12-14.)

Part of the grace of God is that he will empower us to do his works. We can share his power and authority.

The apostle Paul cautions, "And no man taketh this honour unto himself, but he that is called of God. . . ." (Hebrews 5:4.) That is, God will call and delegate his power to whom he will. Man cannot conjure up the power himself nor can he give it to himself. It is a gift of God. The Lord made this clear to those to whom he gave his power and authority in the meridian of time when he said: "Ye have not chosen me, but I have chosen you, and ordained you, . . . that whatsoever ye shall ask of the Father in my name, he may give it you." (John 15:16.) The Lord calls; man responds and is the recipient of God's goodness.

Those who attempt to follow Jesus are indebted to the senior apostle of his day, Peter, for giving a name to the power and authority of God as delegated to man. He called the power and authority of God as given to man "priesthood" or "holy priesthood." (1 Peter 2:5, 9.) Jesus said that he ordained Peter and his associates. (John 15:16.) Peter said that such call and ordination made of them a "priesthood, . . . the people of God." (1 Peter 2:9-10.) The Lord ordains and gives his power for the use of man.

In an ancient instruction on priesthood, we read, "And it was delivered unto men by the calling of his own voice, according to his own will, unto as many as believed on his name." (Inspired Version, Genesis 14:28-29.)

The apostle Paul, in his enlightening epistle to the Hebrew saints, discusses priesthood in some detail, referring to those called to the priesthood as "holy brethren, partakers of the heavenly calling." (Hebrews 3:1.) He says that those called to this holy order are properly called sons of God, and that men called to the priesthood are "ordained . . . in things pertaining to God." (Hebrews 5:1.) But most importantly, Paul teaches us that even Jesus Christ was called to hold the holy priesthood: ". . . consider the Apostle and High Priest of our profession, Christ Jesus. . . ." (Hebrews 3:1.) Jesus was "called of God an high priest after the order of Melchisedec." (Hebrews 5:10.)

As in all matters pertaining to salvation, Jesus was a perfect example. He is the sole perfect exemplar, the prototype of our salvation. As he was baptized, so must we be baptized. (John 3:5; 2 Nephi 31:12-21.) As he received the holy priesthood to merit the fulness of salvation, so must those who would be joint heirs with him also receive the holy priesthood. (D&C 107:5, 8, 18-19.) In the perfect pattern of life and salvation, "The Lord sware and will not repent, Thou art a priest forever after the order of Melchisedec." (Hebrews 7:21.) Priesthood, the power and authority of God, is intended for man's enjoyment; indeed, it is necessary for man to have it to be saved.

When Jesus promised men that they might do the works that he did, it was with two conditions: (1) they must keep his commandments — "If he do whatsoever I command you"

(John 15:14), and (2) they must ask in the Lord's name —
"Whatsoever ye shall ask in my name, that will I do" (John
14:13). In early days the name of God's priesthood was "the
Holy Priesthood, after the Order of the Son of God." (D&C
107:3.) Thus, it is by the proper use of his priesthood that one
may act in his name.

As there is only one God and thus only one power of God,
it must follow that there is only one priesthood. It is "the Holy
Priesthood, after the Order of the Son of God." (D&C 107:3.)
We are taught that "out of respect or reverence to the name of
the Supreme Being, to avoid the too frequent repetition of his
name, they, the church, in ancient days, called that priesthood after Melchizedek, or the Melchizedek Priesthood."
(D&C 107:4.) Thus, in the epistle to the Hebrews we read
repeatedly of the order known as the Melchizedek Priesthood. The Prophet Joseph Smith taught that "all Priesthood is
Melchizedek, but there are different portions or degrees of
it." (Joseph Fielding Smith, comp., *Teachings of the Prophet
Joseph Smith* [Salt Lake City: Deseret Book Co., 1976], p. 180.)
He further said: "Its institution was prior to 'the foundation of
this earth, or the morning stars sang together, or the Sons of
God shouted for joy,' and is the highest and holiest Priesthood, and is after the order of the Son of God, and all other
Priesthoods are only parts, ramifications, powers and
blessings belonging to the same, and are held, controlled, and
directed by it." (Ibid., p. 167.)

Priesthood is the eternal power and authority of God by
which all things were created and are now controlled. As
pertaining to our existence and experience, it is the power and
authority of God delegated to man on earth to act in all
matters pertaining to the salvation of man on the earth. Everything in the heavens and the earth is subject to the power and
authority of the priesthood.

In The Church of Jesus Christ of Latter-day Saints there
are two great orders of the priesthood: the Melchizedek
Priesthood and the Aaronic Priesthood. The Aaronic Priest-

hood is an appendage to the Melchizedek Priesthood. That is, the Melchizedek Priesthood includes all powers and authorities exercised in the Aaronic order. When it is understood that one is talking of orders within God's priesthood, it is generally accepted usage to say that there are two priesthoods in the Church. Hence, the revealed statement: "There are, in the church, two priesthoods, namely, the Melchizedek and Aaronic, including the Levitical Priesthood." (D&C 107:1.) The Prophet Joseph Smith explains that the "Melchizedek Priesthood comprehends the Aaronic or Levitical Priesthood. . . ." (*Teachings*, p. 166.)

In our day we are indebted to the Prophet Joseph Smith for much of our understanding about the priesthood and its reality in our lives. "The Priesthood is an everlasting principle," he said, "and existed with God from eternity, and will to eternity, without beginning of days or end of years." (Ibid., pp. 157-58, 323.) Adam and others had the priesthood conferred upon them "in the Creation, before the world was formed." (Ibid., p. 157.) Alma says that those "ordained unto the high priesthood of the holy order of God" were "called and prepared from the foundation of the world according to the foreknowledge of God" to enjoy the blessings and powers of the priesthood. (Alma 13:7, 3.)

Righteousness and the Priesthood

Righteousness results from obedience to the laws and ordinances of the gospel. The Lord said to those whom he had called to his priesthood, " . . . if ye do whatsoever I command you . . . whatsoever ye shall ask of the Father in my name, he may give it you." (John 15:14, 16.)

No person is wholly righteous. However, by walking in the light of the gospel and obeying the celestial law to the extent of one's ability, one may attain a high degree of righteousness. In the beatitudes Jesus said: "Blessed are they which do hunger and thirst after righteousness: for they shall be filled." (Matthew 5:6.)

God is the very embodiment of righteousness. "Righteousness" is one of his names. Christ is sometimes called Son of Righteousness. (2 Nephi 26:9; 3 Nephi 25:2; Ether 9:22.) The state of righteousness is a state of godliness.

There is an inseparable blessing between righteousness and the powers and blessings of the priesthood.

Two of the great functions of the priesthood are to learn and to teach of God and his ways. With direct reference to priesthood offices the Lord says, "I am your lawgiver. . . . I say unto you, teach one another according to the office wherewith I have appointed you." (D&C 38:22-23.) Priesthood quorums and functions provide the means of instruction and teaching one another. The priesthood further "holdeth the key of the mysteries of the kingdom, even the key of the knowledge of God. . . . And without . . . the authority of the priesthood, the power of godliness is not manifest unto men in the flesh." (D&C 84:19-21.)

" . . . let every man esteem his brother as himself." (D&C 38:24.) This is an important part of priesthood function. We are brethren, children of the same Father, members "of the household of God." (Ephesians 2:19.) Priesthood concept and practice should develop brotherly love.

From the same scriptural text we read, " . . . practice virtue and holiness before me." (D&C 38:24.) Priesthood is more than precept; it is also example. Teaching, learning, and loving are not enough. All of this must be translated into action. This, too, is priesthood function. Priesthood is given to us to the end that we shall act out God's purposes.

To further these ends, we are organized into units, or quorums, so we can act in concert, be more effective, and accomplish more righteousness.

The practice of holiness and power is the practice of priesthood. God's initial priesthood fiat still holds forth:

That every one being ordained after this order and calling should have power, by faith, to break mountains, to divide the seas, to dry up waters, to turn them out of their course;

To put at defiance the armies of nations, to divide the earth, to break every hand, to stand in the presence of God; to do all things according to his will, according to his command, subdue principalities and powers; and this by the will of the Son of God which was from before the foundation of the world. (Inspired Version, Genesis 14:30-31.)

This is what Jesus was talking about when he said to those whom he had called to priesthood callings, "The works that I do shall ye do also; and greater works than these shall ye do... in my name." (John 14:12-13.)

In 1839 the Prophet Joseph Smith expressed in prayer his soul-felt yearnings: "O God, where art thou? And where is the pavilion that covereth thy hiding place? How long shall thy hand be stayed, and thine eye, yea, thy pure eye, behold from the external heavens the wrongs of thy people and of thy servants. . . . Remember thy suffering saints, O our God. . . ." The answer from the Lord was sure: "My son, peace be unto thy soul; thine adversity and thine afflictions shall be but a small moment." (D&C 121:1, 2, 6, 7.) Then came one of the most sublime revelations on priesthood ever recorded:

How long can rolling waters remain impure? What power shall stay the heavens? As well might man stretch forth his puny arm to stop the Missouri river in its decreed course, or to turn it up stream, as to hinder the Almighty from pouring down knowledge from heaven upon the heads of the Latter-day Saints.

Behold, there are many called, but few are chosen. And why are they not chosen?

Because their hearts are set so much upon the things of this world, and aspire to the honors of men, that they do not learn this one lesson —

That the rights of the priesthood are inseparably connected with the powers of heaven, and that the powers of heaven cannot be controlled nor handled only upon the principles of righteousness.

That they might be conferred upon us, it is true; but when we undertake to cover our sins, or to gratify our pride, our vain ambition, or to exercise control or dominion or compulsion upon the souls of the children of men, in any degree of unrighteousness, behold, the heavens withdraw themselves; the Spirit of the Lord is grieved; and when it is withdrawn, Amen to the priesthood or the authority of that man.

Behold, ere he is aware, he is left unto himself, to kick against the pricks, to persecute the saints, and to fight against God.

We have learned by sad experience that it is the nature and disposition of almost all men, as soon as they get a little authority, as they suppose, they will immediately begin to exercise unrighteous dominion.

Hence many are called, but few are chosen.

No power or influence can or ought to be maintained by virtue of the priesthood, only by persuasion, by long-suffering, by gentleness and meekness, and by love unfeigned;

By kindness, and pure knowledge, which shall greatly enlarge the soul without hypocrisy, and without guile —

Reproving betimes with sharpness, when moved upon by the Holy Ghost; and then showing forth afterwards an increase of love toward him whom thou hast reproved, lest he esteem thee to be his enemy;

That he may know that thy faithfulness is stronger than the cords of death.

Let thy bowels also be full of charity towards all men, and to the household of faith, and let virtue garnish thy thoughts unceasingly; then shall thy confidence wax strong in the presence of God; and the doctrine of the priesthood shall distil upon thy soul as the dews from heaven.

The Holy Ghost shall be thy constant companion, and thy scepter an unchanging scepter of righteousness and truth; and thy dominion shall be an everlasting dominion, and without compulsory means it shall flow unto thee forever and ever. (D&C 121:33-46.)

No man fully understands priesthood. It is eternal, "having neither beginning of days, nor end of life." (Hebrews 7:3.) Its power is without bounds. (Matthew 28:18.) Finite mind cannot comprehend infinite and eternal priesthood. God, in his goodness, magnifies man. He gives him his priesthood, and, as we shall see, through it he makes available to man "all that my Father hath." (D&C 84:38.)

Examples of Men Doing God's Work

Through priestly power, the works that the Lord performed during his earthly ministry were continued by his chosen and ordained servants. Peter was chief among them. After Jesus' ascension into heaven, Peter continued his good works in Jesus' name.

Now Peter and John went up together into the temple at the hour of prayer, being the ninth hour.

And a certain man lame from his mother's womb was carried, whom they laid daily at the gate of the temple which is called Beautiful, to ask alms of them that entered into the temple;

Who seeing Peter and John about to go into the temple asked an alms.

And Peter, fastening his eyes upon him with John, said, Look on us.

And he gave heed unto them, expecting to receive something of them.

Then Peter said, Silver and gold have I none; but such as I have give I thee: In the name of Jesus Christ of Nazareth rise up and walk.

And he took him by the right hand, and lifted him up: and immediately his feet and ancle bones received strength.

And he leaping up stood, and walked, and entered with them into the temple, walking, and leaping, and praising God. (Acts 3:1-8.)

This was not the fervent prayer of a righteous man. It was a priesthood directive: "Rise up and walk." It was a command in the name of the Lord. Jesus had promised, "The works that

I do shall he do also . . . in my name." (John 14:12-13.) The Lord's power and authority remained on the earth.

As the Lord's priesthood continues in our day, so his work continues in our day. A member of the Quorum of the Twelve Apostles in the restored church was given first-person testimony of the continuation of the Lord's work today. Elder Matthew Cowley said the following in an address at Brigham Young University on February 18, 1953:

I've told the story about the little baby nine months old who was born blind. The father came up with him one Sunday and said, "Brother Cowley, our baby hasn't been blessed yet; we'd like you to bless him."

I said, "Why have you waited so long?"

"Oh, we just didn't get around to it."

Now, that's the native way; I like that. Just don't get around to doing things! Why not live and enjoy it? I said, "All right, what's the name?" So he told me the name, and I was just going to start when he said, "By the way, give him his vision when you give him a name. He was born blind." Well, it shocked me, but then I said to myself, why not? Christ told his disciples when he left them they could work miracles. And I had faith in that father's faith. After I gave that child its name, I finally got around to giving it its vision. That boy's about twelve years old now. The last time I was back there I was afraid to inquire about him. I was sure he had gone blind again. That's the way my faith works sometimes. So I asked the branch president about him. And he said, "Brother Cowley, the worst thing you ever did was to bless that child to receive his vision. He's the meanest kid in the neighborhood, always getting into mischief." Boy, I was thrilled about that kid getting into mischief! . . .

I was called to a home in a little village in New Zealand one day. There the Relief Society sisters were preparing the body of one of our Saints. They had placed his body in front of the Big House, as they called it, the house where the people came to wail and weep and mourn over the dead, when in rushed the dead man's brother.

He said, "Administer to him."

And the young natives said, "Why, you shouldn't do that; he's dead."

"You do it!"

This same old man that I had with me when his niece was so ill was there. The younger native got down on his knees, and he anointed the dead man. Then this great old sage got down and blessed him and commanded him to rise. You should have seen the Relief Society sisters scatter. And he sat up, and he said, "Send for the elders; I don't feel very well." . . . we told him he had just been administered to, and he said: "Oh, that was it." He said, "I was dead. I could feel life coming back into me just like a blanket unrolling." Now, he outlived the brother that came in and told us to administer to him. (*Matthew Cowley Speaks* [Deseret Book Co., 1954], pp. 247-49.)

The apostle Paul catalogued some of the good works performed through faith by ancient priesthood bearers. In his monumental epistle on priesthood to the Hebrew saints, in the eleventh chapter of Hebrews, this most articulate of New Testament writers wrote of his Old Testament brethren who "wrought righteousness" and "blessed . . . concerning things to come" and "obtained promises" by exercising God's own power. He started his recounting with the first man's son, saying that through faith, "Abel offered unto God a more excellent sacrifice." Then he cited instance after instance that appeared in the Old Testament as simple historical narratives and declared that they were performed with the power of the Son of God. He said that Enoch was translated by this power. Noah acted through it. Abraham sought the heavenly city (the translated city of Enoch) through it. Sarah conceived a child "because she judged him faithful who had promised" in priesthood blessing. Isaac blessed Jacob, and Jacob blessed his sons through this agency. Moses, "esteeming the reproach of Christ greater riches than the treasures of Egypt," acted in His power and authority in keeping the priesthood ordinances, "the passover, and the sprinkling of blood," and by this power "passed through the Red sea as by dry land." It was through faithful use of his power that "the walls of Jericho fell down." Paul says, "Time would fail me to tell of Gideon, and of Barak, and of Samson, and of Jephthae; of David also, and Samuel, and of the prophets: Who through faith subdued kingdoms, wrought righteousness, obtained promises, stopped the mouths of lions, Quenched the violence of fire." (This is a reference to Melchizedek himself, who, as a child, feared God, stopped the mouths of lions, and quenched the violence of fire, according to the Inspired Version, Hebrews 11.)

It was never intended that God share his priestly power with only an elite few. One of the purposes of the scriptures is to encourage us all to be worthy so we may enjoy this sharing. Moses gave voice to the yearnings of all who enjoy this power in his prayer: "Enviest thou for my sake? would God that all the Lord's people were prophets, and that the Lord would put his spirit upon them!" (Numbers 11:29.)

Through scriptural examples and life experiences, the Latter-day Saints are encompassed about, like Paul, with a cloud of witnesses. Most of us have experienced the beauty of God's sharing his power with us. This is joy! This is rapture! Sometimes there is drama. In terms of man's wisdom and puny abilities it is always miraculous.

May I add my personal witness by way of testimony. I have seen the terminally sick made well by the power of God, exercised by his legal administrators. I recall, almost by random selection, the following illustration of our Lord's goodness in fulfilling his promise that "he that believeth on me, the works that I do shall he do also. . . . And whatsoever ye shall ask in my name, that will I do." (John 14:12-13.) Late one evening, the phone rang in the mission home. One of our district leaders was phoning to tell me how sick an elder in his district was. I knew the missionary had a history of muscle spasms that resulted in uncontrollable hiccups. When this had happened before, the doctor had prescribed muscle relaxants, and the spasms had stopped. He also said that if the medication did not stop the spasms, there was nothing medical science could do. That night the medicine had no effect, and the muscle spasms continued for hour after hour, wracking the young elder's stomach and chest with pain. He had not been able to eat, drink, or sleep for nearly twenty-four hours.

I told the district leader to bring the missionary to the home. When they arrived I turned to the district leader and said, "You are a priesthood bearer. Anoint him." He anointed the elder with consecrated oil, and I was voice in sealing the anointing. There was sweet, peaceful assurance. God's power was there, and the still small voice whispered instructions. As the words were spoken, directing the young man to breathe normally, the spasms stopped. The Lord healed him as our hands were on his head. I know that God manifests his power in what is done righteously and properly in his name.

The Church is administered constantly by and through the delegated power and authority of God. I call it operational inspiration. While I was a presiding officer over a small portion of Church affairs, we held a press conference for the president of the Church at the Arizona Temple visitors center. The first question was asked by a sharp-minded young reporter: "Mr. Kimball, you were introduced as the president of The Church of Jesus Christ of Latter-day Saints and also as a prophet. My question is: Does God speak to you? And if so, how?" President Spencer W. Kimball, senior apostle on the earth, responded: "Yes. God speaks to his prophets today, just as he spoke to his prophets yesterday and just as he will speak to them tomorrow. You will remember that Amos wrote, 'Surely the Lord God will do nothing, but he revealeth his secret unto his servants the prophets.' (Amos 3:7.) Sometimes he speaks with an audible voice. Sometimes he sends his angels, as he did to Joseph, the stepfather of Jesus. Usually it is by the still small voice of God to the spirit within. Yes. Have I answered your question, young man?"

Most of the time the use of God's power and authority is not attended by high drama, important as the work is. The Lord's work is to save people. When a priest in the Aaronic Priesthood performs the ordinance of baptism by immersion in water, he is doing the work of the Lord. It is written: "When therefore the Pharisees had heard that Jesus made and baptized more disciples than John . . . though he himself baptized not so many as his disciples." (Inspired Version, John 4:1, 3.) As Jesus baptized, so may we baptize in his name. As we follow his example, we do his works. The world needs righteous models. The sons of God, priesthood bearers, are to be lights upon a hill. "As with the people, so with the priest" (Isaiah 24:2) and "like people, like priest" (Hosea 4:9).

God cannot fail. All of his work will succeed. Righteousness will prevail. It follows that all who are engaged in righteous endeavors will ultimately succeed. In his statement addressed to those "who are the called according to his purpose," which includes priesthood bearers, the apostle Paul said, "And we know that all things work together for the good to them that love God." (Romans 8:28.)

CHAPTER TWO

The Aaronic Priesthood

Adam was the first man on the earth. He was the first person to whom God gave his priesthood. (Moses 6:67-68.) This priesthood continued with his worthy descendants until the day of Moses. (D&C 84:5-16; 107:41-53.) Through Moses, the Lord attempted to set up the house of Israel as a kingdom of priests of the holy order, with each man and his family enjoying the full blessings of the patriarchal order and priesthood. (Exodus 19:5-6; Deuteronomy 26:18.) But Israel rebelled and rejected the higher law, and the Lord took Moses and the fulness of the priesthood from them. (Inspired Version, Exodus 34:1-2; D&C 84:17-25.) For the most part, the scriptures are accounts of the Lord's dealings with his servants, the priesthood bearers.

One of the most significant misconceptions in worldly

scholarship has to do with the notion of the developing concept of God in the history of mankind. It is widely believed that as civilizations developed, so also man's idea about God developed, and man's understanding about God is now superior to his understanding about God in ancient times. This is interesting sociological theory. It is also false. According to this theory, the earliest religion, which included the worship of many gods, came into being as part of the evolutionary development of man. The concept of one supreme Deity was gradually accepted by the Hebrew peoples according to this theory. This concept simply is not true. It is not only not in accord with all revealed scripture, but it is also directly contrary to the scriptural presentation of the history of God's dealings with mankind.

Many of the writings of inspired men from the old world have been handed down from age to age and preserved for us in the Bible. As these writings were originally given, they were the mind and will of God and his voice to all who would listen. (D&C 68:4.) The major characters therein "saw the God of Israel" (Exodus 24:10), and, as one of the most preeminent authors of the Old Testament said, "And the Lord spake unto Moses face to face, as a man speaketh unto his friend." (Exodus 33:11.) The biblical accounts of God's creation of heaven and earth and his association with and revelations to Adam and the patriarchs are true, so far as they have been correctly translated. (Article of Faith 3.) This has all been reconfirmed by direct revelations by God in this day. For instance, the Book of Moses and the Book of Abraham, both in the Pearl of Great Price, set forth the truth about God's ancient dealings with the people from the days of Adam down; the Book of Mormon establishes the divinity of such ancient prophets as Isaiah; and many direct revelations to Joseph Smith outline God's dealings with his ancient Saints. (D&C 84 and 107.)

When God revealed the fulness of the gospel to Moses, he called Moses to his holy order of priesthood. Not many people in the history of mankind have been more intimately acquainted with God than was Moses. God also revealed knowledge about himself and his power and his saving truths to such prophets as Adam, Enoch (Moses 6 and 7), Noah (Moses 8), and Abraham (Abraham 2:6-11; Galatians 3:6-8, 18.) Moses, like the prophets just cited, was the head of a great dispensation of the gospel. (D&C 84:17-28.)

The Israelites whom Moses was called to lead out of bondage were not prepared for a fulness of the gospel. Because they rebelled and manifested gross unworthiness, God took from them the power whereby they could have become a kingdom of priests and kings. That is, he took the fulness of the gospel from them. He substituted the lesser law and called it the "law of carnal commandments."

And the Lord said unto Moses, "Hew thee two other tables of stone, like unto the first, and I will write upon them also, the words of the law, according as they were written at the first on the tables which thou brakest; but it shall not be according to the first, for I will take away the priesthood out of their midst; therefore my holy order, and the ordinances thereof, shall not go before them; for my presence shall not go up in their midst, lest I destroy them.

"But I will give unto them the law as at the first, but it shall be after the law of a carnal commandment; for I have sworn in my wrath, that they shall not enter into my presence, into my rest, in the days of their pilgrimage. . . ." (Inspired Version, Exodus 34:1-2.)

This is what the apostle Paul was talking about in his epistle to the Galatian saints when he explained that God gave the gospel to Abraham and that thereafter the law "was added because of transgressions." (Galatians 3.) He told the Hebrew saints that their fathers had had the fulness of the gospel, but it "did not profit them" because of unbelief. (Hebrews 4:1-5.)

The law of carnal commandments was given to prepare Israel, after more than four hundred years in Egyptian slavery, for the fulness of the gospel. It was to be a schoolmaster:

"Wherefore the law was our schoolmaster to bring us unto Christ. . . ." (Galatians 3:24.) They were the "divers washings, and carnal ordinances, imposed on them until the time of reformation." (Hebrews 9:10.) They are recorded in great detail in Exodus, Leviticus, Numbers, and Deuteronomy, some of Moses' writings in the Old Testament. They were also preserved on the brass plates which the Nephites took with them. (1 Nephi 4:15-16.)

The Book of Mormon prophet Abinadi taught that the law of Moses was given to point the attention of the people forward to Christ. All of the performances and ordinances "were types of things to come." Israel was given "a very strict law; for they were a stiffnecked people, quick to do iniquity, and slow to remember the Lord their God; Therefore there was a law given them, yea, a law of performances and of ordinances, a law which they were to observe strictly from day to day, to keep them in remembrance of God and their duty towards him." (Mosiah 13:29-31.) It was called "the law of carnal commandments" (D&C 84:27; Hebrews 7:16) because it was given to teach those belonging to a chosen lineage to bridle their passions, to overcome the lusts of the flesh, to triumph over carnal things, and to advance to a place where the Spirit of the Lord could have place in their hearts.

Nephi said simply that the law of Moses was given to prove to the people "the truth of the coming of Christ; for, for this end hath the law of Moses been given; and all things which have been given of God from the beginning of the world, unto man, are the typifying of him." (2 Nephi 11:4.)

The great lawgiver Moses gave more than the law of carnal commandments. It was also his responsibility to lead his people to Christ. He also received and recorded many gospel truths, which are eternal in nature and have been in force in all dispensations. The Ten Commandments are part of "the law of Christ." (D&C 88:21.)

When the Lord gave the law of carnal commandments, he gave a lesser order of priesthood to administer this lesser law.

(Hebrews 7:12.) This lesser priesthood was conferred upon Aaron and his sons after him. (Exodus 28, 29, and 30; Leviticus 1:11, 3:2, and 13:2; Numbers 18.) It was given as "an everlasting priesthood throughout their generations." (Exodus 40:15; Numbers 25:10-13.)

Who Was Aaron?

Aaron was the oldest son of Amram and Jochebed of the tribe of Levi. (Exodus 6:16-23.) He was three years older than his brother Moses (Exodus 7:7) and younger than his sister Miriam. He married Elisheba, a woman of the tribe of Judah, by whom he had four sons: Nadab, Abihu, Eleazar, and Ithamar. (Exodus 6:23.)

The Lord appointed Aaron the spokesman of Moses and instructed him to meet Moses in the wilderness. (Exodus 4:27.) In Israel's first recorded battle with the Amalekites, Aaron and Hur supported the hands of Moses. (Exodus 17:10-12.) Aaron held a position of prominence and leadership among the elders. (Exodus 18:12.)

Aaron held the Melchizedek Priesthood. (John Taylor, *Items on Priesthood* [1881], p. 5.) With two of his sons, Nadab and Abihu, as well as Moses and seventy of the elders of Israel, Aaron "saw the God of Israel." (Exodus 24:9-10.) When Moses "went up into the mount of God," Aaron and Hur were left in a position of presidency over the other elders. (Exodus 24.)

At Sinai, while Moses was on the mount receiving the law, Aaron granted the request of the people that they should have a God whom they could see in their corruption. The idol was in the form of an Egyptian deity, the Apis-bull. (Exodus 32:22-25, 35.)

Aaron's family was selected for the lesser priesthood, which priesthood was made hereditary (Exodus 28), and Aaron became the head of this priestly order. Thus to Aaron went the honor, as a memorial to him in all generations, of having his name used to identify the lesser, Levitical, or Aaronic Priesthood. (D&C 84:18-27; 107:1, 20.) Aaron and his sons were chosen to bear that priesthood by which the lesser law was administered. (Numbers 16:3-10, 40.) Aaron's position then became comparable to that of the presiding bishop of The Church of Jesus Christ of Latter-day Saints. (John Taylor, *op. cit.*, pp. 5-6.) After the beginning of the Aaronic order, Aaron and his sons after him were anointed priests unto Israel. (Exodus 28, 29, and 30; Numbers 3 and 4.)

Aaron's sons Nadab and Abihu were destroyed for unholy conduct. (Leviticus 10:1-3.) Aaron and Miriam were not always supportive of Moses; for her criticism of Moses, Miriam was smitten with leprosy. (Numbers 12.)

A staff carried by Aaron was known as Aaron's rod. When it was thrown down in the presence of Pharoah, it became a snake. (Exodus 7:9-12, 15.) During sedition in the wilderness it budded as a sign of divine approval of Moses and Aaron. (Numbers 17:1-10.) It was preserved in the ark. (Hebrews 9:4.)

On Mount Hor, in the sight of all the congregation, Aaron's priestly robes were transferred to his son Eleazar, who succeeded him. Aaron left this world at the age of 123 years. (Numbers 20:23-29; 33:39.) He has ever since been honored as the first head of the Aaronic Priesthood.

Aaron is not a leader without human weaknesses. An objective overview of his mission and life brings him into view as one of the most worthy and venerated leaders in Israel's history. This is attested to by the more than 325 specific references to him in the Old Testament. He was a colorful character. His physical appearance was legendary; King David sang of it: ". . .even Aaron's beard: that went down to the skirts of his garments." (Psalm 133:2.) Perhaps it is his humanness that encourages the rest of us who follow after his order to emulate his successes. His life, like the priesthood that bears his name, helps weak mortals. It shows the spiritual heights to which we can ascend, imperfect, jealous, and stubborn though we are. Aaron shows us that though a man may wrongly fashion a golden calf, he may also repent and be accepted of God, and that God will stand by him and allow him in His presence.

It is recorded that Aaron died on Mount Hor (Numbers 33:39), and maybe that is what happened. However, while it was recorded of Moses that he died and was buried by the hand of the Lord (Deuteronomy 34:5-7), Alma said that he "was taken up by the Spirit," or, more specifically, "the scriptures saith the Lord took Moses unto himself." (Alma 45:18-19.) Moses was translated, as were many, like strangers and pilgrims on earth before him. (D&C 45:11-14; Hebrews 11:5, 11-16.) There is some scriptural evidence that Aaron parted this probationary state in the same manner as did Moses. The Lord said to Moses, "Get thee up into this mountain. . . . And die in the mount whither thou goest up, and be gathered unto thy people; as Aaron thy brother died in mount Hor, and was gathered unto his people." (Deuteronomy 32:48-50.) Another account of this incident preserves the reference that Moses' leaving of this world was to be like Aaron's: ". . . thou also shalt be gathered unto thy people, as Aaron thy brother was gathered." (Numbers 27:13.) I choose to believe that Aaron was translated as Moses was translated.

Israel mourned Aaron's leaving them for thirty days (Numbers 20:29), but they sang of "Aaron the saint of the Lord" (Psalm 106:16) for generations to come.

The Aaronic Priesthood

The Aaronic Priesthood is a priesthood of great majesty and power. It "is called the lesser priesthood . . . because it is an appendage to the greater, or the Melchizedek Priesthood." (D&C 107:13-14.) The term "lesser priesthood" in no sense is derisive. It is lesser only to the fulness of the power of God. As a part of the power and authority of God delegated to men on the earth, the Aaronic Priesthood represents more power than the combined armies and political systems of men.

The Priesthood of Aaron "has power in administering outward ordinances" (D&C 107:13-14) required for salvation. When one is commissioned in this holy order, he becomes a legal administrator empowered to baptize in the name of the "Father, and of the Son, and of the Holy Ghost." (D&C 20:73.) God delegates to those in this order of his priesthood the agency to act for and in his behalf.

The Priesthood of Aaron "holds the keys . . . of the gospel of repentance." (D&C 13.) It is a preparatory priesthood because it is given to prepare people to accept the gospel. Inasmuch as Elias was the harbinger of Jesus Christ, the Priesthood of Aaron is sometimes referred to as the Priesthood of Elias. Repentance is the key to one's preparation to know God. Therefore, the Aaronic Priesthood holds the keys of the gospel of repentance.

The Priesthood of Aaron "holds the keys of . . . baptism by immersion for the remission of sins." (D&C 13.) Within the Aaronic Priesthood is the authority to baptize, an essential ordinance for salvation. (John 3:5.) Thus, in a literal way, the Aaronic Priesthood helps administer salvation. "The priest's duty is to . . . baptize." (D&C 20:46.)

The Priesthood of Aaron "holds the keys of the ministering of angels." (D&C 13.) This means that those who hold this power of God and are faithful have the key whereby they can open the door to the visitations of God's messengers, the angels.

Teaching and expounding the preparatory gospel as well as exhorting in righteousness are within the purview of the Aaronic Priesthood. "The priest's duty is to preach, teach, expound, exhort." (D&C 20:46.)

The opportunity to "administer the sacrament" is given to the Aaronic Priesthood. (D&C 20:46.) Members of the Aaronic Priesthood are also to "watch over the church always, and be with and strengthen" the members; to "see that there is no iniquity in the church"; and to "take the lead of meetings." (D&C 20:53-54, 56.) "Every . . . priest, teacher, or deacon is to be ordained according to the gifts and callings of God unto him." (D&C 20:60.)

Members of this order are to be involved in the basic teaching programs of the Church; they are to "visit the house of each member, and exhort them to pray vocally and in secret and attend to all family duties." (D&C 20:47.)

Aaronic Priesthood bearers are under obligation to participate in the priesthood missionary work of the Church. They are to "invite all to come unto Christ." (D&C 20:59.)

Aaron was the first head of the priesthood that bears his name. He was "called of God" (Hebrews 5:4) to this position of God's power. When the Lord first gave the law of carnal commandments as preparatory gospel, he gave a preparatory power in priesthood to administer the lesser law. (Hebrews 7:12; Inspired Version, Exodus 34:1-2.) This lesser priesthood was conferred upon Aaron and his sons after him. (Exodus 28, 29, and 30; Leviticus 1:11, 3:2, 13:2; Numbers 18.)

Later the Aaronic Priesthood was conferred upon substantially all of the men of the tribes of Levi. Those who were between thirty and fifty years of age were given specific priestly duties in the tabernacle. (Numbers 4:2-4.) Sometimes this order of priesthood is called the Levitical Priesthood. In this dispensation the terms Aaronic Priesthood and Levitical Priesthood are used interchangeably. (D&C 107:1, 6, 10.)

The ancient holders of the Aaronic Priesthood administered numerous ordinances and performances, which are set forth and described in considerable detail in the books of the law (Exodus, Leviticus, Numbers, and Deuteronomy). The apostle Paul referred to these many duties as "diverse washings, and carnal ordinances." (Hebrews 9:10.) He described them as "the law of commandments contained in ordinances." (Ephesians 2:15.)

The purpose of these numerous ordinances was to help school an unruly people to the end that they could accept the Holy One of Israel. An illustration of how these performances and demonstrations were used to center people's attention on the Lord is found in the standard Moses was directed to raise on a pole:

> And the Lord said unto Moses, Make thee a fiery serpent, and set it upon a pole: and it shall come to pass, that every one that is bitten, when he looketh upon it, shall live.
> And Moses made a serpent of brass, and put it upon a pole, and it came to pass, that if a serpent had bitten any man, when he beheld the serpent of brass, he lived. (Numbers 21:8-9.)

As the Israelites wandered in the desert, many were bitten by poisonous serpents. Moses directed them to look up to a standard he raised and live. Many refused, and they died of poison. Those who obeyed were taught to look to a standard and have faith, and they lived. Alma commented on this:

> Behold, [the Son of God] was spoken of by Moses; yea, and behold a type was raised up in the wilderness, that whosoever would look upon it might live. And many did look and live.
> But few understood the meaning of those things, and this because of the hardness of their hearts. . . . they would not look, therefore they perished. (Alma 33:19-20.)

Helaman makes the meaning even plainer:

> Yea, did he not bear record that the Son of God should come? And as he lifted up the brazen serpent in the wilderness, even so shall he be lifted up who should come.
> And as many as should look upon that serpent should live, even so as many as should look upon the Son of God with faith, having a contrite spirit, might live, even unto that life which is eternal. (Helaman 8:14-15.)

John taught the same lesson in the New Testament times, saying, ". . . as Moses lifted up the serpent in the wilderness, even so must the Son of man be lifted up." (John 3:14.) Thus were types and performances used as teaching aids, as a schoolmaster to bring people to an understanding of the person and message of Jesus Christ. In Abinadi's words, they "were types of things to come." (Mosiah 13:31.)

Since all of this was administered under the direction of the Aaronic Priesthood, those chosen to this order were likely to be prominent people in Israel. God honors certain persons by giving them a portion of his power and authority known as the Aaronic Priesthood.

From Aaron to John the Baptist

Soon after the consecration of Aaron and his sons, the Lord announced a major expansion of those to whom he would give his power and authority. He directed Moses and Aaron to make a census of all the male members of Israel "from twenty years old and upward" (Numbers 1:2-3), except one of the twelve tribes was not to be included in the count: "Only thou shalt not number the tribe of Levi, neither take the sum of them among the children of Israel" (Numbers 1:49). These were to be appointed to look after "the tabernacle of testimony, and over all the vessels thereof, and over all things that belong to it. . . ." (Numbers 1:50.) They were no longer numbered as a separate tribe of Israel. The Lord said to Moses:

Bring the tribe of Levi near, and present them before Aaron the priest, that they may minister unto him.

And they shall keep his charge, and the charge of the whole congregation before the tabernacle of the congregation, to do the service of the tabernacle.

And they shall keep all the instruments of the tabernacle of the congregation, and the charge of the children of Israel, to do the service of the tabernacle.

And thou shalt give the Levites unto Aaron and to his sons: they are wholly given unto him out of the children of Israel. (Numbers 3:6-9.)

Aaron's Call a Prototype

Ever since Aaron was called and ordained to the priesthood, the procedure and source of his calling have been cited as being an authoritative and exemplary call. Paul used the example of Aaron in his instruction on how to properly obtain priesthood power and authority: "And no man taketh this honour unto himself, but he that is called of God, as was Aaron," he said. (Hebrews 5:4.) Aaron's call was the perfect precedent. He was called by God, through God's legal administrator on earth, and then authoritatively ordained to the office of his calling. All of this was carefully preserved for us in the Bible.

The Lord directed Moses, "And take thou unto thee Aaron thy brother, and his sons with him, from among the children of Israel, that he may minister unto me in the priest's office, even Aaron, Nadab and Abihu, Eleazar and Ithamar, Aaron's sons. . . . And thou shalt . . . anoint them, and consecrate them, and sanctify them, that they may minister unto me in the priest's office. . . . it shall be a statute forever unto him and his seed after him." (Exodus 28:1, 41, 43.)

Indeed it has been a statute for men. This is the way it is done today. One who represents God, an ordained and set-apart bishop, calls a worthy neophite and confers upon him the Aaronic order of the priesthood of God.

The Lord continued his instructions to Moses: "And thou shalt anoint them, as thou didst anoint their father, that they may minister unto me in the priest's office: for their anointing shall surely be an everlasting priesthood throughout their generations." (Exodus 40:15.)

It was a perfect call and ordination because it had its inception in God. This was and is God's way. Moses, God's earthly administrator, simply executed divine directives. "Thus did Moses: according to all that the Lord commanded him, so did he." (Exodus 40:16.)

It was never intended that this order of the priesthood would be conferred only upon one man and his sons. Approximately 17,160 of the men of Israel (Numbers 4) were initially "called of God, as was Aaron" (Hebrews 5:4.) Once again the record is clear. "And the Lord spake unto Moses, saying, Bring the tribe of Levi near, and present them before Aaron the priest, that they may minister unto him." (Numbers 3:5-6. See also Numbers 3 and 4.) The Aaronic Priesthood was conferred upon substantially the whole male membership of the house of Levi.

The Lord preserved the record for us. It sets forth the perfect prototype. Where substantially identical procedure is followed today, there is God's holy order. It was to this end that the record was kept, that in the mouth of more than one witness, truth can be established. (Deuteronomy 19:15; John 8:13-18.)

As Joshua said of the Aaronic Priesthood bearers of his day, "For the priesthood of the Lord is their inheritance" (Joshua 18:7), so also it may be said of those in our day who have been called of God, as was Aaron.

The Lord confirmed this in a personal revelation to Aaron: "I have taken your brethren the Levites . . . : to you they are given as a gift for the Lord. . . ." (Numbers 18:6.) And so from the beginning the bearers of the priesthood were "as a gift for the Lord."

The Levites operated under the direction of the Aaronic Priesthood and they did not have the fulness that Aaron and his sons held. ". . . their Priesthood was only an appendage to the Aaronic Priesthood, and not that Priesthood itself as held by Aaron and his sons." (Taylor, *Items on Priesthood*, p. 43.) The Aaronic or Levitical Priesthood is one priesthood. (Smith, *Doctrines of Salvation* 3:86.) In those early days there was a difference in function within this priesthood, but in our day the terms are used interchangeably. (D&C 107:1, 6.)

We cannot be certain from the scriptural citations as to the exact age or time when a Levite could enter the priesthood. Certain Aaronic Priesthood functions were assigned "from thirty years old and upward even unto fifty years old, every one that entereth into the service." (Numbers 4:43.) It would appear that there were great numbers of men so to serve. (Numbers 4:36, 40, 44; Genesis 46:11.)

The Levites did not receive a land inheritance as did the other Israelites. "Thou shalt have no inheritance in their land, neither shalt thou have any part among them: I am thy part and thine inheritance among the children of Israel." (Numbers 18:20.) The priesthood was their inheritance. "But the Levites have no part among you; for the priesthood of the Lord is their inheritance. . . ." (Joshua 18:7.) However, their physical wants and needs were cared for. (Numbers 18:21-24; 35:2-3.)

The establishment of the Aaronic Priesthood was all done under the direction of the incomparable Moses. So great was Moses that even Christ is described as a prophet like unto this leader of all of Israel's hosts. (Deuteronomy 18:15-19; Acts 3:22-23; 3 Nephi 20:23.) Although Aaron held the keys of leadership for the Aaronic Priesthood for nearly forty years, this was not the power and authority from God by which Israel was governed during this time. It was to Moses that God said, "I have made thee a god . . . and Aaron thy brother shall be thy prophet." (Exodus 7:1.) Moses, with the fulness of the priesthood, was the presiding officer of his day. ". . . the Melchizedek Priesthood was greater than the Aaronic, and . . . while it ruled, it controlled all matters pertaining to the government and instruction of the people, and . . . it organized and directed the Aaronic Priesthood which was in reality an appendage to the greater." (Taylor, *Items on Priesthood*, p. 11.) The Aaronic Priesthood cannot preside in the presence of the Melchizedek Priesthood. While Moses lived, all priesthood activity was under his direction. He prepared the sons of Aaron and the Levites to take over when he would leave them.

Aaron and his sons acted in the full power of the Aaronic Priesthood. Many of their functions would be comparable to the duties of the bishops and priests in The Church of Jesus Christ of Latter-day Saints today.

The righteous Levites had the right to hold the power and authority of God. Of them Paul writes, "They that are of the sons of Levi, who receive the office of the priesthood, have a commandment to take tithes of the people according to the law, that is, of their brethren, though they come out of the loins of Abraham." (Hebrews 7:5.) They participated in the offering of sacrifices. Many of their functions were comparable to those of teachers and deacons in this dispensation. (Numbers 3 and 4; 2 Chronicles 29; Malachi 3:3.)

Shortly after the death of Aaron, the Lord was ready to take away the fulness of his "holy order, and the ordinances thereof" (Inspired Version, Exodus 34:1), as he said he would. In fulfillment of prophecy, Moses and the higher laws were taken from Israel:

Therefore, he took Moses out of their midst, and the Holy Priesthood also;

And the lesser priesthood continued, which priesthood holdeth the key of the ministering of angels and the preparatory gospel;

Which gospel is the gospel of repentance and of baptism, and the remission of sins, and the law of carnal commandments, which the Lord in his wrath caused to continue with the house of Aaron among the children of Israel until John, whom God raised up, being filled with the Holy Ghost from his mother's womb. (D&C 84:25-27.)

"Until John," referring to John the Baptist, meant that the sacrificial offerings of Israel would be directed by the Aaronic Priesthood from the death of Moses until the time of John the Baptist. At that time Jesus Christ would come and bring the Mosaic dispensation to an end. The sons of Aaron and the Levites were properly called and trained. They were ready to preside as well as function otherwise when Moses was taken from them.

The Prophet Joseph Smith was once asked, "Was the Priesthood of Melchizedek taken away when Moses died?"

He answered: "All Priesthood is Melchizedek, but there are different portions or degrees of it. That portion which brought Moses to speak with God face to face was taken away; but that which brought the ministry of angels remained." (*Teachings,* pp. 180-81.) That portion which remained was the Aaronic or Levitical Priesthood.

"And the Lord confirmed a priesthood also upon Aaron and his seed, throughout all their generations...." (D&C 84:18.) This was the priesthood in general usage in ancient Israel. It was hereditary; that is, it was disseminated by virtue of who one's father and mother were. From Aaron to John the Baptist the hereditary nature of the Levitical Priesthood was in active operation. (D&C 84:18, 26-27, 30; *Teachings,* pp. 318-19.) This order of priesthood was conferred only upon the worthy members of the special lineage chosen to receive it.

The taking of the Melchizedek Priesthood from Israel meant that the bearers of the higher priesthood would not be among them in as great a number. It did not mean that the said power and authority of God would not be among them in any form. Prophets of God, clothed with his authority and the fulness of his priesthood, worked with Israel. (Smith, *Doctrines of Salvation* 3:84-85.)

However, from that time until the time of Christ it was the Aaronic Priesthood that directed the detail and the functions of the law of Moses. When Moses was taken, Eleazar and the Aaronic Priesthood began to bear rule in Israel. (See Lee A. Palmer, *Aaronic Priesthood Through the Centuries* [Deseret Book, 1964], for a detailed account of the Aaronic Priesthood from Aaron to John.)

John the Baptist was a descendant of Aaron (*Teachings,* pp. 272-73) and held the keys of the Aaronic Priesthood. Zacharias, his father, was a priest of God and officiated in the temple. "John was a priest after his father, and held the keys of the Aaronic Priesthood, and was called of God to preach the Gospel of the kingdom of God." (Ibid.) John received a special ordination: "For he was baptized while he was yet in his childhood, and was ordained by the angel of God at the time he was eight days old unto this power, to overthrow the kingdom of the Jews, and to make straight the way of the Lord before the face of his people, to prepare them for the coming of the Lord, in whose hand is given all power." (D&C 84:28.)

John was the last legal administrator holding the keys of the Aaronic Priesthood in the Mosaic dispensation. (D&C 84:26-28.) He had the keys of the Aaronic Priesthood, and although he was a priest, his position, like that of Aaron before him, was comparable to the office of the presiding bishop in his Aaronic Priesthood responsibilities.

This order of the priesthood was given of God to prepare the way of the Lord. It is the Priesthood of Elias, that is, a preparatory priesthood. (D&C 84:107.) "The spirit of Elias is to prepare the way for a greater revelation of God, which is the Priesthood of Elias, or the Priesthood that Aaron was ordained unto. And when God sends a man into the world to prepare for a greater work, holding the keys of the power of Elias, it was called the doctrine of Elias, even from the early ages of the world." (*Teachings*, pp. 335-36.) This is the office and calling of the priesthood John held. He was great because he magnified his office in the priesthood. Of this priest in the Aaronic Priesthood, the Lord said, "Among those that are born of women there is not a greater prophet than John the Baptist. . . ." (Luke 7:28.)

Righteous Pride

When serving on my first mission, I was assigned to Aquidneck Island, Rhode Island, a small island off the coast of New England in the Atlantic Ocean. We were teaching a small group of nonmembers in a weekly cottage meeting. Each week the missionaries would present a gospel subject, entertain questions, and lead a discussion.

One of the young ladies impressed me as a person of quality and refinement. She wasn't aloof, but she was separate from the others. Her bearing was different, almost regal. One could feel her sense of self-confidence.

At the conclusion of one of the lessons I asked her if she knew what set her apart from the others. "Yes," she said. "Don't you know who my father is?" I had no idea who her father was and told her so. She said, "My father is a descendant of Levi. He has traced his lineage to Levi, of the house of Israel." My silence and, I suppose, blank expression prompted her to continue her explanation. "My father is not a religious man," she said. "He goes to the synagogue only on special holy days. But when he goes, the rabbi always steps aside and asks him if he will participate in the service, read the scriptures, or the like." I still did not understand. "He has the right, don't you see?" My countenance brightened. "My father holds the Levitical Priesthood by right of birth. I am set apart from my associates!"

Think of that! It has been 2,000 years since the Mosaic dispensation, with its priesthood of father and mother, ended with John the Baptist, and yet here was a young woman who felt a distinction, almost as of royalty, because her father was of the lineage that once enjoyed the inheritance of the Aaronic Priesthood.

I thought, Oh, that we who have been honored to bear this order of the priesthood in the Dispensation of the Fulness of Times could feel the righteous pride of the call from God, as was Aaron.

A brief incident in the life of a modern apostle and prominent statesman illustrates the awe in which he stood of priesthood calling.

Reed Smoot was the first Latter-day Saint to represent Utah in the United States Senate, serving in that august body for nearly a quarter of a century. During that time he was an ordained apostle in priesthood calling and was a set-apart member of the Counsel of the Twelve Apostles. He became the chairman of the Senate Appropriations Committee and was one of the key opinion makers and policy setters in the United States.

He was a respected and powerful leader of the political party to which he owed allegiance. When his party met in Chicago to name its nominee for the office of president, he was a leader of the convention. His party had won the presidency the last several elections, and most observers thought the trend would continue. It was almost conceded that this convention would name the next president of the United States.

Senator Smoot met in a hotel room with the power structure of the party to choose the man they could all support. Reporters representing the news media of the world were waiting in the hall. At one point in the deliberations Senator Smoot opened the door and made a statement in the presence of the newspaper men that has since come into standard political parlance. He said, "I can't stand decisions made in smoke-filled rooms."

During this convention the leaders assembled there said to Senator Smoot, "Senator, you may have the nomination if you want it. There is one stipulation: You will have to soft-peddle the fact that you are a Mormon." Senator Smoot is reported to have replied, "I would rather be a deacon in The Church of Jesus Christ of Latter-day Saints than be president of the United States."

This is reminiscent of the psalmist saying, "I had rather be a doorkeeper in the house of my God, than to dwell in the tents of wickedness." (Psalm 84:10.) The spiritual sovereign is superior to the temporal sovereign.

CHAPTER THREE

Purchasing a Good Degree

The apostle Paul captures the essence of the purpose of the Aaronic Priesthood in discussing the qualifications for the office of a deacon in the early Church. He wrote these instructions:

Likewise must the deacons be grave, not doubletongued, not given to much wine, not greedy of filthy lucre;

Holding the mystery of the faith in a pure conscience. *And let these also first be proved*; then let them use the office of a deacon, being found blameless.

For they that have used the office of a deacon well purchase to themselves a good degree, and great boldness in the faith which is in Christ Jesus. (1 Timothy 3:8-10, 13. Italics added.)

35

We are thus authoritatively advised that the Aaronic Priesthood offices are preparatory in nature, a proving grounds, positions of training and apprenticeship. They are to be used to prepare persons for greater boldness in the faith, for service in a more abundant dispensing of God's own power and authority.

Before one can understand the discussion that follows on the responsibilities of those who hold offices within the Aaronic Priesthood, he must understand that this order of the priesthood was established to teach and train. Indeed, the greatness of the Aaronic order is that it prepares one for and helps one associate with the glories of the fulness of the power and authority of God as delegated to man on the earth, which is the Melchizedek Priesthood.

The Church of Jesus Christ of Latter-day Saints is operated by the Melchizedek Priesthood. Everything it does is by that agency:

All other authorities or offices in the church are appendages to this priesthood.

The Melchizedek Priesthood holds the right of presidency, and has power and authority over all the offices in the church in all ages of the world, to administer in spiritual things.

The power and authority of the higher, or Melchizedek Priesthood, is to hold the keys of all the spiritual blessings of the church —

To have the privilege of receiving the mysteries of the kingdom of heaven, to have the heavens opened unto them, to commune with the general assembly and church of the Firstborn, and to enjoy the communion and presence of God the Father, and Jesus the mediator of the new covenant. (D&C 107:5, 8, 18-19.)

When He reigns whose right it is to reign, everything on earth will be subject to His power and authority. Even under present circumstances everyone ordained after Christ's order and calling should have power, by faith, to do all things according to his will. And the Aaronic Priesthood is an essential part of the helps and governments established to help us reach this enviable position.

The Aaronic Priesthood recipient is an assistant to one holding the Melchizedek Priesthood, while the fundamental responsibility of the Melchizedek Priesthood is to perfect the Saints so they can see the face of God.

An apt scriptural illustration as to how it is intended that officers of the Aaronic Priesthood will assist the officers of the Melchizedek Priesthood is found in the revelation on Church organization and government:

The duty of the elders, priests, teachers, deacons, and members of the church of Christ — An apostle is an elder, and it is his calling to baptize;

And to ordain other elders, priests, teachers, and deacons;

And to administer bread and wine — the emblems of the flesh and blood of Christ —

And to confirm those who are baptized into the church, by the laying on of hands for the baptism of fire and the Holy Ghost, according to the scriptures;

And to teach, expound, exhort, baptize, and watch over the church;

And to confirm the church by the laying on of the hands, and the giving of the Holy Ghost;

And to take the lead of all meetings.

The elders are to conduct the meetings as they are led by the Holy Ghost, according to the commandments and revelations of God.

The priest's duty is to preach, teach, expound, exhort, and baptize, and administer the sacrament,

And visit the house of each member, and exhort them to pray vocally and in secret and attend to all family duties.

And he may also ordain other priests, teachers, and deacons.

And he is to take the lead of meetings when there is no elder present;

But when there is an elder present, he is only to preach, teach, expound, exhort, and baptize,

And visit the house of each member, exhorting them to pray vocally and in secret and attend to all family duties.

In all these duties the priest is to assist the elder if occasion requires. (D&C 20:38-52.)

The elders in the Melchizedek Priesthood have the duty to watch over the Church. They are to conduct meetings, baptize, confirm those baptized into the Church, teach and exhort, administer the emblems of the sacrament, confer the priesthood to others and ordain to offices therein, and generally take the lead in church administration. In many of these priestly functions the priests, teachers, and deacons in the Aaronic Priesthood are to assist the elders.

Watching over the Church, with all that that portends, is a function of the Melchizedek Priesthood. The Lord uses members of the Aaronic Priesthood, in the nature of on-the-job training, to assist and thus serve and enjoy learning experiences and growth. In subsequent chapters, the revealed duties of the several offices within the Aaronic Priesthood are discussed. To be properly understood, all of this must be seen in the context of overall Melchizedek Priesthood superintendence and ultimate responsibility.

For instance, it is the elders' responsibility to baptize and administer the sacrament. Priests are accorded the singular honor of participating in performing these ordinances. It is the elders' responsibility to watch over the Church. Teachers are specifically empowered to assist them in this particular calling. (D&C 20:53.) Thus teachers may participate in the home teaching and welfare programs of the Melchizedek Priesthood, though not as equal partners. It is a Melchizedek Priesthood function to warn the world, to teach, and to testify (D&C 42:12; 88:81); however, deacons and teachers and priests are specifically directed to participate in missionary activity (D&C 20:59). And so it is with all of the Aaronic Priesthood offerings unto the Lord in righteousness. In all of the functions pertaining to salvation, the Melchizedek Priesthood leads the way. In many of these functions the Aaronic Priesthood has a part. Those who utilize its functions and prerogatives are on the Lord's errand, too.

Prospective Elders

Because it is the purpose of the Melchizedek Priesthood to help the membership of the Church "enjoy the communion and presence of God," all adult male members of the Church who are not ordained elders are considered prospective elders. "A prospective elder is an adult male member of the Church, nineteen years of age or older, who does not hold the Melchizedek Priesthood." (*Melchizedek Priesthood Handbook*, 1975, p. 2.) Many of these men now hold the Aaronic Priesthood. "All prospective elders may be ordained priests as soon as their worthiness permits. It is not necessary to first ordain them deacons or teachers." (Ibid., p. 21.)

From the phrase "prospective elder" one may discern that in the Church system of things, the Aaronic Priesthood is thought of as a preparatory order for the Melchizedek Priesthood. This is in complete harmony with the same order of things in both the New Testament and Old Testament.

Part of the helps and governments the Church affords its members today is the prospective elders program. In this program the president of the elders quorum is responsible for "any family headed by an Aaronic Priesthood member" and "unmarried adult male members who do not hold the priesthood and who are not living at home." (Ibid., p. 11.)

All of the advantages incident to quorum brotherhood are given the prospective elder in the elders quorum. "Prospective elders join with elders for quorum meeting instruction and all appropriate social activities and service projects." (Ibid., p. 2.)

Aaronic Priesthood brethren who are considered prospective elders participate with the elders in priesthood responsibilities. "Elders quorums should be given the responsibility for home teaching all prospective elders and their families, and where feasible should use prospective elders who hold the Aaronic Priesthood to assist them. The basic responsibility of the bishop for home teaching remains the same." (First Presidency letter, January 1972). Thus the administration of the Church procedure implements the precept enunciated by Paul.

The prospective elders program is an interim program to bring persons to the fulness of God's power. President Spencer W. Kimball declared: "As the bishops discharge their duties as president of the Aaronic Priesthood in their wards, the prospective elders program should fade out. We hail that day!" (Address at MIA June Conference, June 23, 1974.)

The Aaronic Priesthood offices are to be used to develop the bearer of the Priesthood of Aaron into something better — "purchasing a good degree."

CHAPTER FOUR

"Upon You I Confer the Priesthood of Aaron"

In eloquent simplicity the Prophet Joseph Smith recorded in his diary the events of the restoration of the Aaronic Priesthood. At the time, the Prophet was translating the plates to be known as the Book of Mormon and dictating to Oliver Cowdery. On the 15th day of May, 1829, the following occurred:

We still continued the work of translation, when in the ensuing month (May, 1829), we on a certain day went into the woods to pray and inquire of the Lord respecting baptism for the remission of sins, that we found mentioned in the translation of the plates. While we were thus employed, praying and calling upon the Lord, a messenger from heaven descended in a cloud of light, and having laid his hands upon us, he ordained us, saying:

Upon you my fellow servants, in the name of Messiah I confer the Priesthood of Aaron, which holds the keys of the ministering of angels, and of the Gospel of repentence, and of baptism by immersion for the remission of sins; and this shall never be taken again from the earth, until the sons of Levi do offer again an offering unto the Lord in righteousness. (D&C 13.)

He said this Aaronic Priesthood had not the power of laying on hands for the gift of the Holy Ghost, but that this should be conferred on us hereafter; and he commanded us to go and be baptized, and gave us directions that I should baptize Oliver Cowdery, and afterwards that he should baptize me. Accordingly we went and were baptized. I baptized him first, and afterwards he baptized me, after which I laid my hands upon his head and ordained him to the Aaronic Priesthood, and afterwards he laid his hands on me and ordained me to the same Priesthood — for so we were commanded.

The messenger who visited us on this occasion, and conferred this Priesthood upon us, said that his name was John, the same that is called John the Baptist in the New Testament. (Joseph Smith, *History of the Church* 1:39-40.)

As in most of the Prophet's writings, he simply puts on record the plain truth pertaining to the coming forth of the work of God. He does not revel in the grandeur of the occasion. For him it is just a simple restatement of events that occurred.

However, Oliver Cowdery was present on this wondrous occasion. He recorded a description of the scene and the impression it left upon his mind. After speaking of his and the Prophet Joseph's desire to be authoritatively baptized, he says:

This was not long desired before it was realized. The Lord, who is rich in mercy, and ever willing to answer the consistent prayer of the humble, after we had called upon him in a fervent manner, aside from the abodes of men, condescended to manifest to us His will. On a sudden, as from the midst of eternity, the voice of the Redeemer spake peace to us, while the veil was parted and the angel of God came down clothed with glory and delivered the anxiously looked for message, and the keys of the Gospel of repentance. What joy! what wonder! what amazement! While the world was racked and distracted — while millions were groping as the blind for the wall, and while all men were resting upon uncertainty, as a general mass, our eyes beheld — our ears heard. As in the "blaze of day;" yes, more — above the glitter of the May sunbeam, which then shed its brilliancy over the face of nature! Then his voice, though mild, pierced to the center, and his words, "I am thy fellow-servant," dispelled every fear. We listened, we gazed, we admired! 'Twas the voice of an angel from glory — 'twas a message from the Most High, and as we heard we rejoiced, while His love enkindled upon our souls, and we were rapt in the vision of the Almighty! Where was room for doubt? Nowhere; uncertainty had fled, doubt had sunk, no more to rise, while fiction and deception had fled forever. But, dear brother, think further, think for a moment what joy filled our hearts and with what surprise we must have bowed, (for who would not have bowed the knee for such a blessing?) when we received under his hands the Holy Priesthood, as he said, 'Upon you my fellow servants, in the name of Messiah, I confer this Priesthood and this author-ity, which remain upon earth, that the sons of Levi may yet offer an offering unto the Lord in righteousness!'

I shall not attempt to paint to you the feelings of this heart, nor the majestic beauty and glory which surrounded us on this occasion; but you will believe me when I say, that earth, nor men, with the eloquence of time, cannot begin to clothe language in as interesting and sublime a manner as this holy personage. No; nor has this earth power to give the joy, to bestow the peace, or comprehend the wisdom which was contained in each sentence as it was delivered by the power of the Holy Spirit! Man may deceive his fellow man; deception may follow deception, and the children of the wicked one may have power to seduce the foolish and untaught, till naught but fiction feeds the many, and the fruit of falsehood carries in its current the giddy to the grave, but one touch with the finger of his love, yes, one ray of glory from the upper world, or one word from the mouth of the Savior, from the bosom of eternity, strikes it all into insignificance, and blots it forever from the mind! The assurance that we were in the presence of an angel; the certainty that we heard the voice of Jesus, and the truth unsullied as it flowed from a pure personage, dictated by the will of God, is to me, past description, and I shall ever look upon this expression of the Savior's goodness with wonder and thanksgiving while I am permitted to tarry, and in those mansions where perfection dwells and sin never comes, I hope to adore in that day which shall never cease. (Ibid., pp. 42-43, footnote.)

John the Baptist, as a resurrected personage, came to Joseph Smith and Oliver Cowdery and made the first conferral of the Aaronic Priesthood in this dispensation. In a further revelation Joseph was reminded: "Which John I have sent unto you, my servants, Joseph Smith, Jun., and Oliver Cowdery, to ordain you unto the first priesthood which you have received, that you might be called and ordained even as Aaron." (D&C 27:8.)

Part of the Restoration of All Things

The visitation of the resurrected John the Baptist and the accompanying conferral of the Aaronic Priesthood is a part of the restoration of all things "which God hath spoken by the mouth of all his holy prophets since the world began." (Acts 3:19-21.) All of the prophets from the beginning of time have looked forward to the dispensation in which we now live, when the work of restoring all saving truths and ordinances is to be accomplished.

The restoration of all things will be accomplished when the earth is restored to that perfect state which prevailed when all things were created, and when the Creator proclaimed that his work was "very good." (Genesis 1:31.) The most important part of the restoration of all things is the restoration of the gospel, of which priesthood restoration was a necessary prerequisite. All of the priesthood and the keys needed to save and exalt mankind in the highest heaven have now been given to us. (D&C 13; 27:12-13; 110:11-16; 128:20-21.)

When the ancient apostle recorded, "And I saw another angel fly in the midst of heaven, having the everlasting gospel to preach unto them that dwell on the earth, and to every nation, and kindred, and tongue, and people" (Revelation 14:6), he was not talking only of the angel Moroni. He saw a composite angel. "Divers angels" (D&C 128:20-21) came in fulfillment of this prophetic vision. John the Baptist was one of them.

As a part of the restoration of all things, certain Levitical ordinances will again be performed in this dispensation, apparently on a one-time basis. In the ordination prayer John the Baptist said that the sons of Levi would make offerings again. (D&C 13.) The offerings that they made in ancient days were sacrifices, and he brought back to earth the commission and the power whereby these ordinances could be performed.

Malachi foretold that such offerings would again be performed in the day of the second coming of Christ. (Malachi 3:1-4.) Joseph Smith wrote:

All the ordinances and duties that ever have been required by the Priesthood, under the directions and commandments of the Almighty in any of the dispensations, shall all be had in the last dispensation, therefore all things had under the authority of the Priesthood at any former period, shall be had again, bringing to pass the restoration spoken of by the mouth of all the Holy Prophets; then shall the sons of Levi offer an acceptable offering to the Lord. . . .

. . . it is generally supposed that sacrifice was entirely done away when the Great Sacrifice (i.e., the sacrifice of the Lord Jesus) was offered up, and that there will be no necessity for the ordinance of sacrifice in [the] future: but those who assert this are certainly not acquainted with the duties, privileges and authority of the priesthood, or with the Prophets.

The offering of sacrifice has ever been connected and forms a part of the duties of the Priesthood. It began with the Priesthood, and will be continued until after the coming of Christ, from generation to generation. We frequently have mention made of the offering of sacrifice by the servants of the Most High in ancient days, prior to the law of Moses; which ordinances will be continued when the Priesthood is restored with all its authority, power and blessings. . . .

These sacrifices, as well as every ordinance belonging to the Priesthood, will, when the Temple of the Lord shall be built, and the sons of Levi be purified, be fully restored and attended to in all their powers, ramifications, and blessings. This ever did and ever will exist when the powers of the Melchisedic Priesthood are sufficiently manifest; else how can the restitution of all things spoken of by the holy Prophets be brought to pass? It is not to be understood that the law of Moses will be established again with all its rites and variety of ceremonies; this has never been spoken of by the Prophets; but those things which existed prior to Moses' day, namely, sacrifice, will be continued. (*History of the Church* 4:210-13.)

Notwithstanding the foregoing, which is yet to be accomplished as part of the restoration of all things, it should be understood that the offering of sacrifices, as a generally practiced ordinance of the gospel, ended with the sacrifice of Christ. The emblems of the sacrament became the newly established ordinance that served the same purpose that sacrifices had heretofore served. The Book of Mormon explains this:

For it is expedient that there should be a great and last sacrifice; yea, not a sacrifice of man neither of beast, neither of any manner of fowl; for it shall not be a human sacrifice; but it must be an infinite and eternal sacrifice.

Now there is not any man that can sacrifice his own blood which will atone for the sins of another. Now, if a man murdereth, behold will our law, which is just, take the life of his brother? I say unto you, Nay.

But the law requireth the life of him who hath murdered; therefore there can be nothing which is short of an infinite atonement which will suffice for the sins of the world.

Therefore, it is expedient that there should be a great and last sacrifice; and then shall there be, or it is expedient there should be, a stop to the shedding of blood; then shall the law of Moses be fulfilled; yea, it shall be all fulfilled, every jot and tittle, and none shall have passed away.

And behold, this is the whole meaning of the law, every whit pointing to that great and last sacrifice; and that great and last sacrifice will be the Son of God, yea, infinite and eternal. (Alma 34:10-14. See also 2 Nephi 2:7.)

The New Testament teaches these same truths, though not in as plain terms. The risen Lord commanded the Nephites: "And ye shall offer up unto me no more the shedding of blood; yea, your sacrifices and your burnt offerings shall be done away, for I will accept none of your sacrifices and your burnt offerings. And ye shall offer for a sacrifice unto me a broken heart and a contrite spirit." (3 Nephi 9:19-20.)

Offices in the Aaronic Priesthood

In the Aaronic Priesthood organization today there are four offices: deacon, teacher, priest, and bishop. Each office is an ordained calling, an assignment to serve. Each office bears a specified area of responsibility.

The priesthood is greater than any of its offices, and no office adds any power or authority to it. All offices derive their rights, prerogatives, power, and authority from the priesthood. No one can hold an office in the priesthood without first holding the priesthood.

Think of the priesthood as a circle:

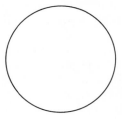

Then envision the offices of the priesthood as segments that make the circle:

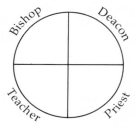

One who serves in one segment must possess the power of the entire circle.

The priesthood is conferred upon selected persons, who are then ordained to offices within the priesthood. Each office in the priesthood is designated as an appendage to the priesthood to which it is attached, and each office is supplemental to the priesthood and grows out of it. (D&C 84:29-30; 107:5; McConkie, *Mormon Doctrine*, pp. 535-37.) Those receiving priesthood office have the obligation to labor with energy as the needs of that ministry require. (D&C 88:109-110; 107:95-100.) Many of the assigned functions of Aaronic Priesthood offices today are comparable to those performed by the Levites of old. (Smith, *Doctrines of Salvation* 3:111-14.)

In New Testament days Aaronic Priesthood bearers entered their ministries when they were young men. This was similar to Old Testament practices. A preeminent apostle in those days, Paul, records in considerable detail the qualification of deacons and their wives and the behavior of their children. (1 Timothy 3:8-13.) When this dispensation commenced, the same pattern was used; the first persons ordained to offices in the Aaronic Priesthood were adult brethren. It is significant that the dispensation in the meridian of times and the dispensation of the fulness of times were officered in part by the offices within the Aaronic order (Philippians 1:1-2), as was also the dispensation of Moses.

We were not far into this dispensation when the preparatory priesthood was given to boys. Joseph Smith's youngest brother "was ordained to the Priesthood when only 14 years of age." (*History of the Church* 4:393.) Since he was subsequently ordained an elder, we know that the priesthood here referred to was of the Aaronic order. (Journal History, July 23, 1833, p. 2.) It is now recommended that "those who are worthy may be ordained to offices in the Aaronic Priesthood at the following minimum ages: Deacon, age 12; Teacher, age 14; Priest, age 16." (*General Handbook of Instructions*, No. 21 [1976], p. 40.)

In order to be called to the priesthood, one must be worthy. The call originates with God and is issued by his servant, the bishop. If the prospective bearer of the priesthood is a minor, the bishop has prior consultation with his parents or guardians to obtain permission. Using the special spiritual gift of discernment, he is to ascertain the worthiness of the neophite. In the *General Handbook of Instructions* we read:

The bishop is to interview carefully every candidate in private to determine his worthiness. The bishop should review with him in detail what will be expected of him as a priesthood holder within a certain office. The review should outline the specific duties in Doctrine and Covenants 20:46-60 as they pertain to the office under consideration. The Aaronic Priesthood member should make a commitment to the bishop that he will continue to —

1. Live the Word of Wisdom, including abstinence from tobacco, alcoholic drinks, coffee, tea, and harmful drugs.

2. Pay a full tithing.

3. Conduct himself with moral cleanliness.

4. Attend to his private prayers, and to regular family prayers if he is head of a family.

5. Fulfill assignments given him by his quorum presidency.

6. Refrain from using the name of the Lord in vain, vulgar expressions, and other forms of degrading language.

7. Honor his parents.

8. Attend priesthood, sacrament, and other meetings.

9. Speak and act honestly.

10. Treat all people with kindness and respect.

11. Do his duty in the Church and live in accordance with its rules and doctrines.

12. Refrain from reading pornographic material or going to pornographic movies.

13. Refrain from the misuse of drugs.

After the interview with the bishop and before being ordained to any office in the Aaronic Priesthood, the name of each candidate is to be presented in sacrament meeting for the sustaining vote of the members. (Ibid.)

After this searching procedure to insure worthiness, the Aaronic Priesthood is conferred upon the person and he is ordained to offices therein under the direction of the bishop. Bishops should encourage worthy fathers to ordain their sons; this is in the patriarchal nature of the ancient order of Aaron.

When a person has been ordained to an office in the Aaronic Priesthood, he is to receive a Certificate of Ordination in the Aaronic Priesthood, which is signed by the bishop and the ward clerk. All ordinations are recorded on the membership records, the ordinance and action records, and the minutes of the Church.

Let us examine the offices within the Aaronic Priesthood in The Church of Jesus Christ of Latter-day Saints.

Deacon

Deacon is one of the ordained offices in the Aaronic Priesthood. (D&C 20:60.) It is the lowest office in the priesthood hierarchy. (D&C 88:127.) However, it represents a very significant office, a high and holy calling in God's kingdom. In order to hold an office in the priesthood, one must have conferred upon him the fulness of that priesthood to which the office is an appendage, and the office of a deacon is an appendage to the Aaronic Priesthood. (D&C 84:30.) Therefore, a deacon holds as much Aaronic Priesthood as does anyone. Others may have more responsibilities and authority to accomplish them but no one holds more of the Aaronic Priesthood than does a deacon.

Deacons are "appointed to watch over the church, to be standing ministers unto the church." (D&C 84:111.) In practice this means that they are at the call of the bishop to minister to the wants of the Church. Included in these responsibilities are such standard assignments as these:

1. Passing the sacrament. Deacons are authorized to pass the emblems of the body and blood of Christ, the sacrament, to members of the Church assembled in worship. They are intimately associated with the heart of our worship services.

2. Gathering fast offerings. Deacons are authorized to gather fast offerings, dedicated donations to the poor. They thus participate in the essence of "pure religion." (James 1:27.)

3. Serving as a messenger for the bishop. Deacons are authorized messengers for the bishop, helping to lighten his load.

4. Caring for the meetinghouse and grounds. Deacons have responsibilities in caring for meetinghouses and grounds, assisting in putting up chairs when needs arise, and a host of service opportunities.

Deacons have the authority and the obligation to assist the ordained teacher "in all his duties in the church, if occasion requires." (D&C 20:57.) They are "to warn, expound, exhort, and teach. . . ." (D&C 20:58-59.) Recall that Noah was given the priesthood when he was ten years old (D&C 107:52), and that "the child Samuel ministered unto the Lord before Eli" and heard the voice of the Lord at a tender age (1 Samuel 3:1-10.) Deacons are to lead exemplary lives and caution associates against all forms of evil. They are to learn the gospel and be able to set forth the precepts thereof.

Deacons are to "invite all to come unto Christ." (D&C 20:59.) They are thus under obligation to be involved in missionary work.

There are some express limitations upon a deacon. They are not to "baptize, administer the sacrament, or lay on hands." (D&C 20:57-60.)

Teacher

Teacher is one of the ordained offices of the Aaronic Priesthood. (D&C 18:32; 20:60.) No biblical passage makes it definite that persons in Old and New Testament times were ordained to the office of a teacher in the priesthood; references to teachers in the Bible may have reference to persons who acted as preachers or instructors. (Acts 13:1; 1 Corinthians 12:28-29; Ephesians 4:11.) However, a teacher was an officer in the New Testament church, as is explained in the sixth Article of Faith: "We believe in the same organization that existed in the Primitive Church, viz., apostles, prophets, pastors, teachers, evangelists, etc." The Prophet Joseph Smith seems to indicate that Christ gave teachers, in an ordained sense, saying, "And how were . . . teachers . . . chosen? By prophecy (revelation) and by laying on of hands . . . through the medium of the Priesthood. . . ." (*Teachings*, p. 206.) The office of teacher appears to be ancient as well as modern in the priesthood.

When a deacon is ordained to the office of a teacher, he does not receive more priesthood. He does receive the right to exercise more of the authority of the Aaronic Priesthood than he was permitted to exercise as a deacon. If one is ordained to the office of a teacher who was not previously ordained to the office of a deacon, the ordination carries with it all of the authority that ordination to the office of a deacon has, plus added appointments and privileges. A teacher continues to exercise the rights and authorities of a deacon. He also has further responsibilities in priestly service.

The office of a teacher is an appendage to the Aaronic Priesthood. (D&C 84:30; 107:5.) Together with the deacons, teachers are appointed "to watch over the church, to be standing ministers unto the church." (D&C 84:111.) As with the deacons, this means that the teacher is at the call of the bishop to minister to the wants of the Church. All of the responsibilities of the office of a deacon are also in the office of a teacher.

The Lord gave to the Prophet Joseph Smith a revelation on Church organization and governance. In legalistic terms this revelation, section 20 of the Doctrine and Covenants, is the "constitution of the Church." The duties of the teacher are therein set out in considerable detail.

The teacher's duty is to watch over the church always, and be with and strengthen them;

And see that there is no iniquity in the church, neither hardness with each other, neither lying, backbiting, nor evil speaking;

And see that the church meet together often, and also see that all the members do their duty.

And he is to take the lead of meetings in the absence of the elder or priest —

And is to be assisted always, in all his duties in the church, by the deacons, if occasion requires.

But neither teachers nor deacons have authority to baptize, administer the sacrament, or lay on hands;

They are, however, to warn, expound, exhort, and teach, and invite all to come unto Christ. (D&C 20:53-59.)

Inasmuch as the responsibilities of the teacher, in large measure, are directed to "the church" it is appropriate to inquire as to what the scriptural definition of "the church" is. Prior to using this term in section 20, the Lord taught Joseph Smith what the terminology meant. He said, "Behold, this is my doctrine — whosoever repenteth and cometh unto me, the same is my church." (D&C 10:67.) That is to say, the church is the people. Again, in the revelation wherein he uses the term "the church" the Lord defines his terms:

All those who humble themselves before God, and desire to be baptized, and come forth with broken hearts and contrite spirits, and witness . . . that they have truly repented of all their sins, and are willing to take upon them the name of Jesus Christ, having a determination to serve him to the end, and truly manifest by their works that they have received of the Spirit of Christ unto the remission of their sins, shall be received by baptism into his church." (D&C 20:37.)

The church is an assembly of congregations of such people.

The teacher is to minister to the wants of God's people. He is to "see that there is no iniquity in the church, neither hardness with each other, neither lying, backbiting, nor evil speaking; . . . and also see that all the members do their duty." (D&C 20:53-55.) Home teaching is one of the assignments given to teachers to enable them to discharge these divinely imposed responsibilities.

The teacher "shall teach the principles of my gospel." (D&C 42:12.) It is expressly stated that the source of his teaching of the gospel shall be the holy scriptures. Implied in this directive is a knowledge through scriptural perusal.

The teacher is given specific instructions to "go to with his might, with the labor of his hands, to prepare and accomplish the things which I have commanded." (D&C 38:40.)

There are some scriptural limitations on the office of a teacher. He does not "have authority to baptize, administer the sacrament, or lay on hands." (D&C 20:58.) His responsibility to do missionary work — "invite all to come unto Christ" (D&C 20:59) — is discussed in more detail later.

The teacher is a significant position in the priesthood structure. When there is no priest or higher authority present he is directed "to take the lead of meetings." (D&C 20:56.) The office is designated by divine fiat as one of leadership.

Priest

A priest is an ordained office in the Aaronic Priesthood. (D&C 18:32; 20:60.) A priest may do all that a deacon or teacher is authorized to do, with additional authority and responsibilities. The duties incident to his calling are some of the most satisfying and important of all priesthood functions. (For a detailed statement of a priest's duties, see Oscar W. McConkie, *The Priest in the Aaronic Priesthood*, published by the Presiding Bishop of the Church.)

This office was instituted at Sinai in a most solemn manner. The Levites there remained true to Jehovah and were chosen for this religious service. (Exodus 32:26-29; Numbers 3:9, 11-13, 40, 41; 8:16-18.) There are more than seven hundred references to the priest in the Bible. The functions of the office of a priest continued into New Testament times. (John 4:1-3.) Baptizing is a function of the priest.

There were ordained priests among the first twenty-seven people in the church in this dispensation. (Joseph Fielding Smith, *Essentials in Church History* [Salt Lake City: Deseret Book Co., 1973], pp. 57-58.)

The Lord outlines the duties of a priest in our day in the basic revelation on church organization and governance:

The priest's duty is to preach, teach, expound, exhort, and baptize, and administer the sacrament,

And visit the house of each member, and exhort them to pray vocally and in secret and attend to all family duties.

And he may also ordain other priests, teachers, and deacons.

And he is to take the lead of meetings when there is no elder present;

But when there is an elder present, he is only to preach, teach, expound, exhort, and baptize,

And visit the house of each member, exhorting them to pray vocally and in secret and attend to all family duties.

In all these duties the priest is to assist the elder if occasion requires. (D&C 20:46-52.)

It is the duty of the priest "to preach, teach, expound, exhort." One of the most satisfying experiences in God's service is to preach under the influence of the Spirit of the Lord. With reference to this specific responsibility of the priest the Prophet Joseph Smith recorded: ". . . if a Priest understands his duty, his calling, and ministry, and preaches by the Holy Ghost, his enjoyment is as great as if he were one of the Presidency; and his services are necessary in the body, as are also those of Teachers and Deacons." (*History of the Church* 2:478.)

"The priest's duty is to . . . baptize." No ordinance is better suited to demonstrate priestly authority than the authorization to baptize. Consider the revealed baptismal prayer: "Having been commissioned of Jesus Christ, I baptize you in the name of the Father, and of the Son, and of the Holy Ghost. Amen." (D&C 20:73.) This is a divine commission, the essence of priesthood usage: the delegation of the authority of God to act for and in his behalf.

"The priest's duty is to . . . administer the sacrament." This means to officiate at the sacrament table and to break the bread and offer the prayers that have been revealed for use in blessing the emblems of the sacrament. In Old Testament times the priests administered the ordinance of sacrifice. Today the priest administers the ordinance reminiscent of the last great sacrifice. The significance of these performances is found in the words of the revealed prayers:

O God, the Eternal Father, we ask thee in the name of thy Son, Jesus Christ, to bless and sanctify this bread to the souls of all those who partake of it, that they may eat in remembrance of the body of thy Son, and witness unto thee, O God, the Eternal Father, that they are willing to take upon them the name of thy Son, and always remember him and keep his commandments which he has given them; that they may always have his Spirit to be with them. Amen. (D&C 20:77.)

O God, the Eternal Father, we ask thee in the name of thy Son, Jesus Christ, to bless and sanctify this wine to the souls of all those who drink of it, that they may do it in remembrance of the blood of thy Son, which was shed for them; that they may witness unto thee, O God, the Eternal Father, that they do always remember him, that they may have his Spirit to be with them. Amen. (D&C 20:79.)

"The priest's duty is to... visit the house of each member." Home teaching is one vehicle to discharge this responsibility. This is a program of the Church where a priesthood bearer goes into the homes of the members and encourages such Christian attributes as prayer.

Priests may "ordain other priests, teachers, and deacons." A priest is authorized to ordain other officers in the Aaronic Priesthood. Once again, this is acting for and in behalf of God.

The priest's duty "is to take the lead of meetings." The priest is herein designated a leader in the household of God.

"In all these duties the priest is to assist the elder if occasion requires." This is a restatement of the truth that the elders in the Melchizedek Priesthood bear the burden of administering all the laws and ordinances of the gospel. Next to the bishop, the priest is the final step in the Aaronic order, the preparatory priesthood. It is he, more than any others, who assists the holders of the higher priesthood.

These three offices of the Aaronic Order — priest, teacher, and deacon — are "to be ordained according to the gifts and callings of God . . . by the power of the Holy Ghost." (D&C 20:60.)

Bishop

Bishop is an ordained office in the Aaronic Priesthood. (D&C 20:67; 107:87-88.) "The office of a Bishop belongs to the lesser Priesthood. He is the highest officer in the Aaronic Priesthood." (Brigham Young, *Journal of Discourses* 9:87.)

The bishop is designated as both the president of the priests quorum and as the president of the Aaronic Priesthood in the area of his jurisdiction. "Also the duty of the president over the Priesthood of Aaron is to preside over forty-eight priests, and sit in council with them, to teach them the duties of their office, as is given in the covenants — This president is to be a bishop; for this is one of the duties of this priesthood." (D&C 107:87-88.)

The office of a bishop is also an appendage "belonging unto the high priesthood." (D&C 84:29.) The bishop is a high priest in the Melchizedek Priesthood as well as an officer in the Aaronic Priesthood. Brigham Young declared: "Can the Bishop baptize the people, according to his Bishopric? He can. When the people he has baptized assemble for confirmation, can he confirm them? He cannot, under the power of his Bishopric; but as he has been ordained to the office of a High Priest, after the order of Melchisedek . . . he has a right as a High Priest to confirm them into the Church by the laying on of hands." (*Journal of Discourses* 9:280.) "The bishop is the presiding high priest in the ward. . . ." (*General Handbook of Instructions*, No. 21 [1976], p. 6.)

"In his Aaronic Priesthood capacity a bishop deals primarily with temporal concerns (D&C 107:68); as the presiding high priest in his ward, however, he presides over all ward affairs and members." (McConkie, *Mormon Doctrine*, p. 89.)

The bishop presides over all members of his ward, regardless of their office or calling.

As is true for all the offices in the priesthood, a bishop is ordained to this calling, a permanent position that he never loses, assuming good behavior. He is set apart to preside in a ward, which is a temporary assignment of presiding.

A bishop is given special spiritual endowments necessary in performing the office of his calling. One of the functions of his office is to act as a common judge in Israel (D&C 107:74), which is an office of judgment. To perform this function, he has a right to have the gift of discernment, which is the power to discern other spiritual gifts, "lest there shall be any among you professing and yet be not of God." (D&C 46:27.)

One indication of the significance accorded the Aaronic Priesthood in the Church today is found in the *General Handbook of Instruction*, the operational manual of the Church: "The bishopric is the presidency of the Aaronic Priesthood in the ward. . . . Their major responsibility is to watch over the young men of the Aaronic Priesthood and the young women of the same age. They are to supervise conferral of and ordinations in the Aaronic Priesthood. They are to emphasize and supervise the Aaronic Priesthood. . . ." (P. 6.)

As far as we are able to tell, the New Testament office of bishop is substantially the same as the office of bishop today. The apostle Paul sets forth these qualifications of a bishop:

> For a bishop must be blameless, as the steward of God; not selfwilled, not soon angry, not given to wine, no striker, not given to filthy lucre;
> But a lover of hospitality, a lover of good men, sober, just, holy, temperate;
> Holding fast the faithful word as he hath been taught, that he may be able by sound doctrine both to exhort and to convince the gainsayers. (Titus 1:7-9.)

These are standard guidelines today in the selection of worthy men for this most special calling.

Presiding Bishop of the Church

It is appropriate to conclude this outline of offices in the Aaronic Priesthood by describing separately the office of a bishop known as the Presiding Bishop of the Church. This is especially appropriate because in this office there may be a continuation of the ancient order of things. This is the office that Aaron held in Old Testament times. Now, as then, the right to this office is hereditary; it descends from worthy father to worthy son: "For the firstborn holds the right of the presidency over this priesthood, and the keys or authority of the same." (D&C 68:17.) In a revelation received by Joseph Smith in 1831 it is recorded: "And if they be literal descendants of Aaron they have a legal right to the bishopric, if they are the firstborn among the sons of Aaron." (D&C 68:16.) To the Priesthood among the Sons of Aaron belongs the legal right to serve as the president of the Aaronic Priesthood and the Presiding Bishop of the Church. This is a living and everlasting monument to Aaron, a "perpetual statute" and "an everlasting priesthood throughout their generations." (Exodus 28:1-3; 40:15.)

The Presiding Bishop is called of God through the mouth of his prophet, the President of the Church. Since he is a General Authority, his is a position of general jurisdiction rather than an office of specific jurisdiction. He holds the keys of presidency over the Aaronic Priesthood of the entire church.

In the absence of a revelation to the President of the Church revealing the lineage of a man to hold this Levitical presidency, the First Presidency is empowered to choose "a high priest of the Melchizedek Priesthood" to hold the office. (D&C 107:17.) All of those chosen thus far in this dispensation have been such high priests.

One who is called by the President of the Church from the loins of Aaron, according to the rule of primogeniture, could serve as Presiding Bishop without counselors. (D&C 107:76.) When the Presiding Bishop is called from among the high priests, he serves with counselors (D&C 107:72), ordained bishops, who are called of God through the Presiding Bishop. These three men, constitute the Presiding Bishopric of the Church. The counselors' authority to act is dependent upon the keys of presidency held by the Presiding Bishop.

The Presiding Bishop may sit as a judge in Israel, to judge transgressors (D&C 107:72), and "none shall be exempted from the justice and the laws of God" (D&C 107:82-84).

He is concerned with and watches over many of the temporal concerns of the church. He is "set apart unto the ministering of temporal things." (D&C 107:71.) The Lord gives him special spiritual insight, "knowledge . . . by the Spirit of truth" (D&C 107:71), to accomplish his calling.

The Presiding Bishop receives consecrations for the care of the Lord's poor. (D&C 42:31-33; 51:5, 12-13.) He is thus intimately associated with the welfare program and its bishop's storehouse. He is also called to travel and preach as an aid to building up the kingdom. (D&C 84:112-116.)

In carrying out the New Testament injunction of bishoprics "to feed the church of God" (Acts 20:28), the Presiding Bishopric sits with the First Presidency of the Church and acts directly under its jurisdiction.

Priesthood Quorums

Those who hold the priesthood are organized into units called quorums. Twelve deacons form a quorum of deacons, twenty-four teachers form a teachers quorum, and forty-eight priests form a quorum of priests. (D&C 107:85-87.)

Each deacons and teachers quorum has a deacon and a teacher, respectively, called to preside over their brethren as president. "Of necessity there are presidents, or presiding officers growing out of, or appointed of or from among those who are ordained to the several offices in these two priesthoods." (D&C 107:21.) The bishop is the president of the priests quorum.

These presidents hold the keys of presidency over the various quorums. It is their obligation to sit in council with their fellow quorum members, "teaching them the duties of their office," "edifying one another, as is given according to the covenants." (D&C 107:85-89.)

The fact that the Lord has chosen quorum organization as the organizational units of his church dramatizes the interdependence of the brethren. Quorums are social, service, and educational units. The quorum furnishes the vehicle for mutual help of its members in every way toward salvation.

Quorums are service units. They are to "give impetus to the service and activities dimension of the Aaronic Priesthood . . . program so that our youth will increase in both their faith and in their capacity to serve their fellowmen. . . . We should not be afraid to ask our youth to render service to their fellowmen or to sacrifice for the kingdom. Our youth have a sense of intrinsic idealism. We need have no fear in appealing to that idealism when we call them to serve. . . . Our youth either know now that 'sacrifice brings forth the blessings of heaven,' or they can come to know that truth, if we will give them greater responsibility and more opportunities for service." (President Spencer W. Kimball, address at MIA June Conference, June 23, 1974.)

The Church gives ever-increasing emphasis to the strengthening of priesthood quorums. President Kimball puts this into proper perspective:

It is our desire to see the quorum presidencies of the Aaronic Priesthood quorums take their tasks seriously, just as we simultaneously are trying to awaken the Melchizedek Priesthood quorums of the Church.

Just as economic and political conditions in the world may give us fresh appreciation for the basics of food, clothing and shelter, and safety, so the Church needs more than ever to focus on fundamentals, like family and quorums.

We must honor the individual, honor the family, honor the quorums, and honor the priesthood. For then we will automatically give more honor and blessings to womanhood.

By focusing on the family and on priesthood quorums — the Aaronic Priesthood and the Melchizedek Priesthood quorums — we can better carry out the unique responsibility of the Church to preach the gospel to every nation in the world; the vitalizing of Aaronic Priesthood quorums and the awakening of the Melchizedek Priesthood quorums will affirmatively affect all other programs in the Church!

We know, of course, that it is change in heart and not change in chart which really makes a lasting difference! I am not discouraged, but I am anxious about my stewardship, just as you should be about yours.

Here we see sparkle the Church teachings wherein the man becomes the child and the child becomes the man through example and training of our superb family life. . . .

If the members of the Church would take giant steps to lift the Church, it must be done or inspired in our families, in our Aaronic Priesthood quorums, in our Melchizedek Priesthood quorums, and in our women programs. (Ibid.)

The great reservoir of power and strength of the sons of God can best be used to its greatest value by having strong, active quorums. As President Harold B. Lee said, "There is no new organization necessary to take care of the needs of this people. All that is necessary is to put the priesthood of God to work. There is nothing you need as a substitute." (General conference address, October 7, 1972.)

The Aaronic Priesthood will remain upon the earth until the day of the second coming of Christ and while he reigns during the Millennium. In ordaining Joseph Smith, John, the heavenly messenger, said of the Priesthood of Aaron, "And this shall never be taken again from the earth, until the sons of Levi do offer again an offering unto the Lord in righteousness." (D&C 13.)

The phrase "the sons of Levi [shall] offer unto the Lord an offering in righteousness" was not original with John the Baptist. It is the phrase used by the prophet Malachi in the last book of the Old Testament as he described the second coming of the Lord: "And he shall sit as a refiner and purifier of silver: and he shall purify the sons of Levi, and purge them as gold and silver, that they may offer unto the Lord an offering in righteousness." (Malachi 3:3.)

"The Priesthood of Aaron, or the Levitical Priesthood, will not end when the sons of Levi make their offering in righteousness, but it will remain on the earth as long as mortals dwell here. . . . As long as we have temporal things on the earth this priesthood is necessary. Eventually, when the earth is celestialized, I suppose all priesthood will be of the higher order." (Smith, *Doctrines of Salvation* 3:91-92.)

CHAPTER FIVE

The Gospel of Repentance

One of the most optimistic and comforting doctrines of Christ is the doctrine of repentance, which is the process of casting off the burden of guilt, the washing away of iniquity and evil, and becoming free from sin. If a person repents, the Lord will not remember his former sins and imperfections. "Behold, he who has repented of his sins, the same is forgiven, and I, the Lord, remember them no more." (D&C 58:42.)

Those who love the Lord and seek to do his will want to cleanse and purify themselves. They want to be pure in heart. It is thus that one becomes a saint. (Mosiah 3:19.) The process of working out one's salvation consists in the cleansing and purifying of one's soul. Men must change from their carnal state to a pure state in which they have been forgiven of their sins. That is, they must be purified through the atoning blood

65

of Christ. (Mosiah 4:2.) The pure in heart shall see God. (Matthew 5:8; 3 Nephi 12:8; D&C 97:16.) They shall be one with Christ (3 Nephi 19:28-29) and shall enjoy exaltation (1 John 3:1-3; Moroni 7:48; D&C 35:21).

Thus we see that the very plan of salvation is based upon the belief in and practice of repentance. Every prophet or inspired teacher in every dispensation has restated Isaiah's dictum: "Wash you, make you clean; put away the evil. . . . Learn to do well." (Isaiah 1:16-17.) This is so fundamental and such an integral part of the gospel that the entire plan of salvation is spoken of as the gospel of repentance. (D&C 13.)

Repentance is essential to salvation. "And we know that all men must repent and believe on the name of Jesus Christ, and worship the Father in his name, and endure in faith on his name to the end, or they cannot be saved in the kingdom of God." (D&C 20:29.) To the end of our own salvation we are commanded to repent, ". . . for, behold, I command all men everywhere to repent." (D&C 18:9-22.)

Now is the time for repentance if we are to have part in the plan of redemption. (Alma 34:31-35.) Peter makes it a directive: "Repent . . . every one of you." (Acts 2:38.)

He who holds the Aaronic Priesthood has two involvements in the process and concept of repentance. He must first concern himself with the process of his own repentance. Then, having commenced to make himself pure in heart, he is under obligation to teach and demonstrate the concept of the gospel of repentance to others.

First Responsibility:
Our Own Repentance

"If we say that we have no sin, we deceive ourselves, and the truth is not in us." (1 John 1:8.) The need for repentance is universal. How do we repent? To answer this question, we must examine each element of the process of repentance. These elements, outlined for us in the scriptures, apply to every member of the Church. They are:

1. Godly sorrow. "For godly sorrow worketh repentance to salvation." (2 Corinthians 7:10.) First, we must recognize the need for repentance in our lives. We must want to escape from the hurtful effects of sin. We must recognize our guilt and be sorry for it. The process of forgiveness starts here.

2. Forsake sin. "By this ye may know if a man repenteth of his sins — behold, he will confess them and forsake them." (D&C 58:43.) One must stop doing what he would be forgiven of. "Cease to do evil." (Isaiah 1:16.)

3. Confession of sins. "I, the Lord, forgive sins unto those who confess their sins before me and ask forgiveness, who have not sinned unto death." (D&C 64:7.) We must always confess our sins to God, to aggrieved persons, and under some circumstances to the Lord's representative, his appointed judge in Israel, under whose jurisdiction we live.

4. Restitution. If one is to repent, he must bring forth "fruits meet for repentance." (Matthew 3:7-9.) He must act consistent with repentance. Restitution to an injured party was a standing law in Israel. (Numbers 5:6-7.) Wherever possible, the wrong must be righted as a part of true repentance. Restitution means restoration, to make amends for the offense committed.

5. Live the law. "He that repents and does the commandments of the Lord shall be forgiven." (D&C 1:32.) The final essential characteristic of true repentance is that the penitent live the law of the gospel. Complete forgiveness is reserved for those who turn their whole hearts to God and begin to keep all of his commandments.

We may repent over and over again, for each sin calls for repentance. However, when we repeat a trespass, we evidence that we really did not repent of it. We do not forsake it. Therefore, each time we sin, repentance becomes more difficult. "I, the Lord, will not lay any sin to your charge; go your ways and sin no more; but unto that soul who sinneth shall the former sins return, saith the Lord your God." (D&C

82:7.) The effects of repentance are thus conditioned upon continued righteousness.

6. Partake of the sacrament. Finally, to gain forgiveness through repentance a person must accept the cleansing power of the blood of Christ as it is offered through the renewal of the baptismal covenants in the sacrament. (D&C 20:75-79; John 6:54.) One receives forgiveness through the Holy Ghost. (3 Nephi 27:19-20.)

Second Responsibility: To Teach and Demonstrate Repentance

Having immersed himself in the process of repentance, the bearer of the Aaronic Priesthood has further responsibility in the gospel of repentance. He must not only be good, but he must also be good for something. He must repent and then teach others to repent.

The holder of this priesthood has a duty "to preach, teach, expound, exhort." Even in the concept of repentance, a priesthood bearer does not worship alone. It is in concert with his fellows that the fulness of the gospel of repentance is realized.

We must be involved in service: service that builds up the kingdom of God from within and service that proselytes others to the cause of truth. We must demonstrate the effects of repentance.

Repentance is such an important aspect of the gospel and its propagation that missionaries are under instruction to "say nothing but repentance unto this generation." (D&C 6:9-11; 11:9.) This means to teach the fundamental principles of the gospel.

Part of the Preparatory Gospel

"And the lesser priesthood . . . holdeth the key of . . . the preparatory gospel; Which gospel is the gospel of repentance. . . ." (D&C 84:26-27.)

The gospel, which is the plan of salvation, embraces all of the laws, principles, doctrines, ordinances, and powers necessary to save and exalt men. The great preparatory principle upon which all of this is based is repentance, and the doctrine of repentance is the preparatory gospel. It is the function of the Aaronic Priesthood to administer the preparatory gospel, to provide the schooling whereby mankind can be led to the gospel of Christ: "The law was our schoolmaster to bring us unto Christ." (Galatians 3:24.) In this important regard the priesthood holder is an officer of the law.

CHAPTER SIX

The Ordinance of Baptism

As the angel ministered to Joseph Smith and Oliver Cowdery on May 15, 1829, he said in part: "Upon you my fellow servants, in the name of Messiah I confer the Priesthood of Aaron, which holds the keys . . . of baptism by immersion for the remission of sins." (D&C 13.)

Baptism by immersion for the remission of sins is a part of preparatory gospel over which the Aaronic Priesthood has jurisdiction. The concepts of faith, repentance, and baptism are spoken of as the preparatory gospel.

When water baptism by immersion is viewed in its historical setting, it is particularly appropriate that it is an Aaronic Priesthood function. God has said that without his ordinances "the power of godliness is not manifest unto men in the flesh." (D&C 84:21.) Jesus is the center of all true religion, and religious ordinances center in him. "And behold, all things have their likeness, and all things are created and made to bear record of me, both things which are temporal, and things which are spiritual." (Moses 6:63.) The Aaronic Priesthood was established to take care of some of God's ordinances. (Hebrews 7:12; Exodus 28, 29, 30; Numbers 3, 4; 2 Chronicles 29; Malachi 3:3.) One of the most important of these ancient rites, the ordinance of sacrifice, is specifically described as being performed in "similitude of the sacrifice of the Only Begotten." (Moses 5:7.)

The ordinance of baptism fits the pattern of other ordinances perfectly. It teaches us of Christ; it centers our attention on him. Paul likens baptism to the death, burial, and resurrection of Jesus. (Romans 6:4-5; Colossians 2:12.) We are thus taught in beautiful symbolism that going into the water and coming forth out of the water are even as his going into the grave and coming forth out of the grave. The ordinance imparts knowledge about God to us.

Baptism is part of the everlasting covenant. It began on earth with Adam (Moses 6:64-67) and has continued ever since whenever the Lord has had a people on earth. (D&C 20:23-28; 84:26-28.) It was not a new rite practiced by John the Baptist and adopted by Christ. The Jews were baptizing their converts long before John. Modern discoveries, such as the Dead Sea Scrolls, have added much light to secular scholarship in the matter of pre-Christian baptisms. The part of the Book of Mormon that deals with the pre-Christian era contains much information relative to this eternal law.

The ordinance of baptism has several characteristics. It has a physical or ceremonial part: being immersed in water. There is a spiritual aspect of the ordinance: having the Holy Ghost ratify that which was done. And finally, through this ordinance one may become sanctified, or achieve a state of holiness and purity. The Lord described these three essential characteristics of baptism to Moses: "For by the water ye keep the commandment; by the Spirit ye are justified, and by the blood ye are sanctified." (Moses 6:60.) One is sanctified by the Spirit because of the blood of Christ. (2 Nephi 27:19-21.)

Baptism is the initiatory ordinance into The Church of Jesus Christ of Latter-day Saints. "No one can be received into the church of Christ unless he has arrived into the years of accountability before God, and is capable of repentance. Baptism is to be administered . . . unto all those who repent." (D&C 20:71-72.)

Baptism is a necessary prerequisite to salvation in the celestial kingdom in the world to come: "And he commandeth all men that they must repent, and be baptized in his name, having perfect faith in the Holy One of Israel, or they cannot be saved in the kingdom of God." (2 Nephi 9:23.)

Both the temporal and spiritual parts of baptism are essential. Of the angelic ministrant's earthly ministry we read:

John did baptize in the wilderness, and preach the baptism of repentance for the remission of sins.

And there went out unto him all the land of Judea, and they of Jerusalem, and were all baptized of him in the river of Jordan, confessing their sins.

And [John] preached, saying: There cometh one mightier than I after me, the latchet of whose shoes I am not worthy to stoop down and unloose.

I indeed have baptized you with water: but he shall baptize you with the Holy Ghost. (Mark 1:4-8. See also Luke 3:16.)

The separable nature of baptism is further illustrated in the ministry of Paul when he met persons who had been baptized "unto John's baptism," that is, water baptism. Paul "laid his hands upon them" and "the Holy Ghost came on them," that is, baptism of the Spirit. (Acts 19:1-6.)

Baptism in water or by immersion is done by the power of the Aaronic Priesthood. (D&C 20:46.) It was thus that John the Baptist was empowered to baptize as he did. (D&C 68:17; 84:26-28.)

Baptism of the Spirit is an administration under the power of the Melchizedek Priesthood. To those holding this priesthood is given authority "to confirm those who are baptized into the church, by the laying on of hands for the baptism of fire and the Holy Ghost." (D&C 20:41.) It was thus that the apostle Paul was able to baptize and confirm as he did.

Baptism means immersion. The meaning of the term at the time of Christ was an actual immersion in water. Contemporary accounts of naval battles in those days spoke of ships being baptized if they were sunk, or partially baptized if they were beached and only partially sunk. (James E. Talmage, *Articles of Faith*, pp. 484-86.) The scriptural accounts of baptism take place in rivers (Mark 1:9) or where there is "much water" (John 3:23).

Modern revelation sets forth in clarity the proper form of baptism:

Baptism is to be administered in the following manner unto all those who repent —

The person who is called of God and has authority from Jesus Christ to baptize, shall go down into the water with the person who has presented himself or herself for baptism, and shall say, calling him or her by name: Having been commissioned of Jesus Christ, I baptize you in the name of the Father, and of the Son, and of the Holy Ghost. Amen.

Then shall he immerse him or her in the water, and come forth again out of the water. (D&C 20:72-74.)

Priests are instruments in the hands of God in performing this essential ordinance.

Purposes of Baptism

The scriptures suggest several purposes served by baptism. First, baptism is a divinely prescribed ordinance for the remission of sins. "Thou shalt declare repentance and faith on the Savior, and remission of sins by baptism, and by fire, yea, even the Holy Ghost." (D&C 19:31.)

Second, baptism admits a repentant person to membership in The Church of Jesus Christ of Latter-day Saints.

All those who humble themselves before God, and desire to be baptized, and come forth with broken hearts and contrite spirits, and witness before the church that they have truly repented of all their sins, and are willing to take upon them the name of Jesus Christ, having a determination to serve him to the end, and truly manifest by their works that they have received of the Spirit of Christ unto the remission of their sins, shall be received by baptism into his church. (D&C 20:37.)

Third, baptism is the gateway — the only way — to the celestial kingdom of heaven. "Except a man be born of water and of the Spirit, he cannot enter into the kingdom of God." (John 3:5.) All men must "be baptized, . . . or they cannot be saved in the kingdom of God." (2 Nephi 9:23.)

Fourth, baptism begins the means of personal sanctification. "Repent, all ye ends of the earth, and come unto me and be baptized in my name, that ye may be sanctified by the reception of the Holy Ghost, that ye may stand spotless before me at the last day." (3 Nephi 27:20.)

The Priest as an Agent of God

Baptism is a sacred contract between God and man, a part of the new and everlasting covenant of the gospel. Each of us who is baptized undertakes certain obligations as our part in this covenant. We agree to serve God and keep his commandments. We are to take upon ourselves the name of Christ. (D&C 18:17-25.) We are to stand as witnesses of God, to bear one another's burdens, and to comfort those that stand in need of comfort and mourn with those that mourn. (Mosiah 8:7-10.)

The Lord, for his part, agrees to "pour out his Spirit" upon those who so contract and assure them of eternal life. The priest who performs this holy ordinance, as the duly commissioned agent of God, performs the function that binds God if the second party to the sacred and solemn contract is faithful and does not breach the agreement.

John the Baptist did not introduce a new rite in his earthly ministry nor when he ministered to Joseph Smith and Oliver Cowdery. A portion of this ordinance has been a part of the ministry of the Aaronic Priesthood since that priesthood was given to the world. Peter, the chief apostle in the New Testament church, put it in plain terms: "He commanded them to be baptized." (Acts 10:48.)

CHAPTER SEVEN

An Offering Unto the Lord in Righteousness

When the Aaronic Priesthood was restored to Joseph Smith and Oliver Cowdery on that momentous day in May 1829, John declared: ". . . and this shall never be taken again from the earth, until the sons of Levi do offer again an offering unto the Lord in righteousness." (D&C 13.)

The prophet Malachi, in the last book of the Old Testament, described the second coming of the Lord: "And he shall sit as a refiner and purifier of silver: and he shall purify the sons of Levi, and purge them as gold and silver, that they may offer unto the Lord an offering in righteousness." (Malachi 3:3.) We are thus assured from the mouth of the restoring angel that the Aaronic Priesthood will remain upon the earth until into the millennium.

Incident to the second coming, and as a part of the restora-

77

tion of all things, certain ancient Levitical ordinances will again be performed in this dispensation. The Prophet Joseph said: "All the ordinances and duties that ever have been required by the Priesthood, under the directions and commandments of the Almighty in any of the dispensations, shall be had in the last dispensation." (*History of the Church* 4:210-11.)

Ceremonial rites or offerings do not fulfill the angelic requirement of offering unto the Lord in righteousness. This offering means much more than ordinance work. There must be a vital, living, and real offering in the lives of the officers in the Aaronic Priesthood.

Making offerings unto the Lord is, in effect, worshiping God: "Thou shalt worship the Lord thy God, and him only shalt thou serve." (Matthew 4:10.) Worship is defined as paying divine honors to deity.

A priesthood bearer may make his offerings in righteousness in putting on himself the Christian disciplines. He thus may worship in paying tithes, in observing the Word of Wisdom and the Sabbath, in fasting, in praying, in his relationship to his family, in his relationship to his community and government, in his total involvement in the Church, in his role in sharing the gospel.

Offerings unto the Lord in righteousness are best made by those who first believe the gospel and join in its outward form and then develop the personal righteousness that makes them the exemplars of the Christian ethic.

Ancient and modern Israel are under commandment to offer their oblations unto the Lord. (Leviticus 7:38; 2 Chronicles 31:14.) In its highest and most meaningful sense, the offering of an oblation consists in giving full devotion unto the Lord. In this dispensation the Lord has directed that our offering unto him be a broken heart and a contrite spirit:

Thou shalt offer a sacrifice unto the Lord thy God in righteousness, even that of a broken heart and a contrite spirit.

For verily this is a day appointed unto you to rest from your labors, and to pay thy devotions unto the Most High;

Nevertheless thy vows shall be offered up in righteousness on all days and at all times;

But remember that on this, the Lord's day, thou shalt offer thine oblations and thy sacraments unto the Most High, confessing thy sins unto thy brethren, and before the Lord. (D&C 59:8, 10-12.)

The priesthood officer in the kingdom is under particular obligation to offer oblations unto the Lord in righteousness. It is thus that he magnifies his priestly calling; it is one important way in which he helps to perfect the Saints.

General Priesthood Functions

Modern revelations outline the specific duties and responsibilities of those holding the Aaronic Priesthood in the church and kingdom of God today. There are also other priesthood functions imposed by scriptures. When the Lord says, "For behold, this is my work and my glory — to bring to pass the immortality and eternal life of man" (Moses 1:39), he is also stating the work of priesthood. The bringing to pass of man's eternal life has been divided into three categories for administrative objectives:

1. Perfect the Saints. To keep the members of the Church in the way of their full duty and to help them walk uprightly before the Lord.
2. Missionary work. To teach the gospel to those who have not yet heard and accepted it.
3. Temple work. To help qualify every member to go to the temple for his own endowments and to have his family sealed to him. To encourage genealogical research and the performance of vicarious temple ordinances so that the worthy dead can participate in the blessings of the gospel. (*Melchizedek Priesthood Handbook*, p. 26).

The Aaronic Priesthood bearer has a priesthood involvement in each of these areas of priesthood administration.

To Preach, Teach, Expound, Exhort

The apostle Paul records that "it pleased God by the foolishness of preaching to save them that believe," and that this is a calling of the brethren. (1 Corinthians 1:21, 26.) Preachers are called of God to teach his saving truths. This has been the case from the beginning. Moses names the patriarchs from Adam to Enoch and describes them, saying: "And they were preachers of righteousness, and spake and prophesied, and called upon all men, everywhere, to repent; and faith was taught unto the children of men." (Moses 6:23.)

This being the order of things, it is necessary that some men be called to perform this essential function. The bearers of the Aaronic Priesthood are among those so called. Paul, the great missionary apostle, explains this concept:

For whosoever shall call upon the name of the Lord shall be saved.

How then shall they call on him in whom they have not believed? and how shall they believe in him of whom they have not heard? and how shall they hear without a preacher?

And how shall they preach, except they be sent? as it is written, How beautiful are the feet of them that preach the gospel of peace, and bring glad tidings of good things!

But they have not all obeyed the gospel. For Esaias saith, Lord, who hath believed our report?

So then faith cometh by hearing, and hearing by the word of God. (Romans 10:13-17.)

Teaching is not only done in formal preachments, but also in informal conversation in many teaching situations. The Lord directs that we should teach in all possible situations:

Hear, O Israel: The Lord our God is one Lord:

And thou shalt love the Lord thy God with all thine heart, and with all thy soul, and with all thy might.

And these words, which I command thee this day, shall be in thine heart:

And thou shalt teach them diligently unto thy children, and shalt talk of them when thou sittest in thine house, and when thou walkest by the way, and when thou liest down, and when thou risest up. (Deuteronomy 6:4-7.)

This great commandment has been repeated in every dispensation. In the dispensation of the fulness of times we have added to the commandment of teaching the principles of the gospel this important statement: "which are in the Bible and the Book of Mormon, in the which is the fulness of the gospel." (D&C 42:12.) Since this commandment was given in 1831 two other standard works have been canonized: the Doctrine and Covenants, and the Pearl of Great Price.

The secret of convincing gospel teaching is given by Nephi: "When a man speaketh by the power of the Holy Ghost the power of the Holy Ghost carrieth it unto the hearts of the children of men." (2 Nephi 33:1.)

The Prophet Joseph Smith, in a revelation specified as the law of the Church, said this about teachers: "And the Spirit shall be given unto you by the prayer of faith; and if ye receive not the Spirit ye shall not teach." (D&C 42:14.)

Before one can properly teach gospel principles, then, he must have the Spirit of the Lord. The priesthood bearer must so live that the Holy Ghost can enlighten his mind and loosen his tongue. He must also know the doctrines of the gospel. "Neither take ye thought beforehand what ye shall say" is the divine decree, "but treasure up in your minds continually the words of life, and it shall be given you in the very hour that portion that shall be meted unto every man." (D&C 84:85. See also Matthew 10:19-20.)

Priesthood bearers who are parents are given special instruction and direction to teach their children:

And again, inasmuch as parents have children in Zion, or in any of her stakes which are organized, that teach them not to understand the doctrine of repentance, faith in Christ the Son of the living God, and of baptism and the gift of the Holy Ghost by the laying on of the hands, when eight years old, the sin be upon the heads of the parents.

For this shall be a law unto the inhabitants of Zion, or in any of her stakes which are organized.

And their children shall be baptized for the remission of their sins when eight years old, and receive the laying on of the hands.

And they shall also teach their children to pray, and to walk uprightly before the Lord." (D&C 68:25-28.)

The art of expounding is a part of the teaching process. To expound is to lay open the meaning of; to set out or expose. Expounding has to do with interpreting and explaining. That which has been said of teaching can be said of expounding.

Expounding gospel principles carries special responsibilities. The priest does not have the prerogative to put his own interpretation on gospel principles. Peter instructs that "no prophecy of the scripture is of any private interpretation." (2 Peter 1:20.) As scriptures are produced when the Holy Ghost moves persons (D&C 68:3-4), so their interpretation must come from the same source (D&C 8:1-2). Thus, in order to discharge his responsibility in expounding, the priesthood bearer must enjoy the companionship of the Holy Ghost.

To exhort is to incite persons to action. It is to advise or to earnestly warn. Exhortation has a particular function in the gospel plan. Paul wrote: "Preach the word; be instant in season, out of season; reprove, . . . exhort with all longsuffering and doctrine." (2 Timothy 4:2.) The purpose of preaching, teaching, and expounding is to motivate our brothers and sisters to righteous action.

One great call to action or exhortation is to earnestly warn the world. "For this is a day of warning, and not a day of many words" (D&C 63:58), and "it becometh every man who hath been warned to warn his neighbor" (D&C 88:81).

In all of these godly purposes the priesthood bearer is an express functionary.

Involvement in Home Teaching

Upon priesthood bearers, including those in the Aaronic Priesthood, rests the obligation to visit the houses of the Saints and to lead the inhabitants thereof to righteousness. This responsibility is detailed in the revelations. Such a teacher's duty is "to watch over the church always, and be with and strengthen them; And see that there is no iniquity in the church, neither hardness with each other, neither lying, backbiting, nor evil speaking." (D&C 20:53-54.)

To aid in the discharge of these responsibilities, the Church sends out priesthood brethren as home teachers to visit the homes of all members at least once a month.

The home teacher represents, first of all, his bishop. This is a solemn responsibility. He should convey the same feeling of love, concern, and interest that the bishop would convey if he were there personally.

Second, he represents his priesthood quorum. The priesthood quorum is the Church unit directly responsible for the welfare of its members, and one of the goals of home teaching is to enrich and develop the feeling of brotherhood within the quorums.

Third, he has the responsibility of coordinating all of the resources of the Church that are necessary to achieve the physical and spiritual needs of his families. The home teacher thus helps to fellowship each family in the wholeness of Church activity. He helps strengthen the home instruction of his family.

Involvement in Church Welfare

The Lord has always been concerned with the temporal welfare of his people. In every dispensation the physical well-being of the people has been a subject of revelation from God. Much of the burden of the prophets and apostles in all ages has been to alleviate social injustices and iniquities.

In this dispensation of the fulness of times the Lord has decreed: "But it is not given that one man should possess that which is above another, wherefore the world lieth in sin." (D&C 49:20.) This is one of the great social pronouncements of all time.

The Lord further spoke to Joseph Smith of the importance of social justice and equality: "You may be equal in the bonds of heavenly things, yea, and earthly things also, for the obtaining of heavenly things. For if ye are not equal in earthly things ye cannot be equal in obtaining heavenly things." (D&C 78:5-6.) Part of the order of the Church was to advance this cause. (D&C 78:4.) Within the organization of the Church was to be "the preparation . . . and the foundation, and the ensample" to eventually accomplish these noble objectives of equality. (D&C 78:13.)

The Lord clearly states his purpose in caring for the physical needs of his people and the penalty of noncompliance to his will:

I, the Lord, stretched out the heavens, and built the earth, my very handiwork; and all things therein are mine.
And it is my purpose to provide for my saints. . . .
For the earth is full, and there is enough and to spare. . . .
Therefore, if any man shall take of the abundance which I have made, and impart not his portion, according to the law of my gospel, unto the poor and the needy, he shall, with the wicked, lift up his eyes in hell. (D&C 104:14-18.)

The bishop is specifically charged with the responsibility of "searching after the poor to administer to their wants." In part this is done by redistributing wealth, or "humbling the rich and the proud." (D&C 84:112.) All of this is under the auspices of the elders. (D&C 20:42.)

Welfare work is not new. Every dispensation has had its tithes, offerings, cooperative enterprises, united orders, planned economies, or whatever arrangements were necessary under the given circumstances. The Church's attempt to apply these divine principles in the daily lives of its members received renewed emphasis in 1936 in a system known as the Church welfare plan.

"Our primary purpose," said the First Presidency, "was to set up, in so far as it might be possible, a system under which the curse of idleness would be done away with, the evils of a dole abolished, and independence, industry, thrift and self respect be once more established amongst our people. The aim of the Church is to help the people to help themselves. Work is to be re-enthroned as the ruling principle of the lives of our Church membership." (*Conference Report*, October 1936, p. 3.)

Part of the responsibility of members of priesthood quorums is to help provide for the temporal well-being of one another. This is part of the brotherhood that membership in the quorum implies.

The quorum itself is to participate in the activities of the welfare program, such as planting, caring for, and harvesting crops, processing foods, storing food, clothing, and fuel, and carrying out other projects for the mutual benefit of its members or other persons.

The relationships of the priesthood with its lofty, unselfish brotherhood, require that quorum members, individually and as groups, exert their utmost means and powers to spiritually and temporally rehabilitate their brothers. The quorum looks upon a needy member as a continuing problem until his temporal and spiritual needs are met. Rehabilitation activities are nearly as many and varied as are the problems. They have included: (1) placing quorum members in permanent jobs; (2) helping the families of quorum members in getting permanent jobs; (3) helping quorum members in trade school training, apprenticeships, and so forth; (4) providing means and encouragement for further schooling; (5) building homes; (6) assisting quorum members in establishing themselves in business.

Caring for one another is not an optional part of the gospel. From the beginning it was intended that we would be our brother's keeper. (Genesis 4:9.) There is hardly a way wherein one could better make an offering unto the Lord in righteousness.

Involvement in Genealogy and Temple Work

An epistle from the Prophet Joseph Smith to The Church of Jesus Christ of Latter-day Saints contains the following reference to offerings to the Lord in righteousness:

Behold, the great day of the Lord is at hand; and who can abide the day of his coming, and who can stand when he appeareth? For he is like a refiner's fire, and like fuller's soap; and he shall sit as a refiner and purifier of silver, and he shall purify the sons of Levi, and purge them as gold and silver, that they may offer unto the Lord an offering in righteousness. Let us, therefore, as a church and a people, and as Latter-day Saints, offer unto the Lord an offering in righteousness; and let us present in his holy temple, when it is finished, a book containing the records of our dead, which shall be worthy of all acceptation. (D&C 128:24.)

The scriptures thus itemize genealogical records for temple work as an offering unto the Lord in righteousness.

One of the great functions of the priesthood is to provide for the dead. "The greatest responsibility in this world that God has laid upon us is to seek after our dead." (*Teachings*, p. 356.) Modern scripture refers to this area of priesthood function as "this most glorious of all subjects belonging to the everlasting gospel." (D&C 128:17.) As such, it represents one of the basic duties imposed upon the Church membership.

"God is not the God of the dead, but of the living." (Matthew 22:32.) That is to say, there is no death nor dead as far as God is concerned. All are alive unto him. The Lord made this statement with reference to Abraham, Isaac, and Jacob, who had died long before as men count death, but who were alive as the Lord views things in his eternal perspective.

In the eternal perspective man's existence and progress from his pre-earth life to his eventual inheritance in one of the post-earth life degrees of glory is one continuing course. In the Lord's view, then, it is not material whether the opportunity to accept the gospel of salvation comes in this mortal sphere or in the world of spirits hereafter. Sometime after birth into this life and before the resurrection and judgment every living soul will hear the gospel message. All will be judged according to the various reactions thereto. The millions who pass, by way of death, into the spirit world without receiving an opportunity during mortality to hear the truths of salvation will receive their chance to hear and accept the gospel.

It was Jesus who organized the missionary work among the spirits in the spirit world: "For Christ also hath once suffered for sins, the just for the unjust, that he might bring us to God, being put to death in the flesh, but quickened by the Spirit: By which also he went and preached unto the spirits in prison; Which sometime were disobedient, when once the long-suffering of God waited in the days of Noah, while the ark was a preparing, wherein few, that is, eight souls were saved by water." (1 Peter 3:18-20.)

The Lord explained this concept: "Marvel not at this: for the hour is coming, in the which all that are in the graves shall hear his voice, And shall come forth; they that have done good, unto the resurrection of life; and they that have done evil, unto the resurrection of damnation." (John 5:28-29.)

The prophets and apostles prophesied of it (Isaiah 42:6-7; 61:1-2) and described its application and procedures in the primitive church (1 Corinthians 15:29).

The principles and procedures whereby the saving truths of the gospel are offered to, accepted by, and made binding upon the departed dead comprise the doctrine of salvation for the dead. That is part of God's plan of salvation. The principles of salvation are taught in the spirit world, leaving the ordinances, which are earthly acts, to be performed in this life on a vicarious or proxy basis. The worthy dead who accept the gospel in the spirit world and for whom the necessary ordinances are performed in this world can become heirs of the fulness of the Father's kingdom. Salvation for the dead is the system under which those who would have accepted the gospel in this life, had they had the opportunity of hearing it, will have the opportunity to accept it in the spirit world and will then be entitled to all the blessings that passed them by in mortality.

One of the evidences that The Church of Jesus Christ of Latter-day Saints is a true restoration of the primitive church established by Christ is that it practices the New Testament doctrine and procedure of baptism for the dead.

"Else what shall they do which are baptized for the dead, if the dead rise not at all? why are they then baptized for the dead?" (1 Corinthians 15:29.)

As in every true application of gospel ordinances, the ordinance of baptism for the dead is an exclusive ordinance of the restored church, administered by authoritative ministers. The rest of the Christian world read of it and wonder.

The administration of the ordinance is a priesthood function, and holders of the priesthood are under a duty to perform the ordinance as a service for our departed dead. We cannot lightly pass over these obligations. (D&C 128:15.)

Young members of the Aaronic Priesthood should participate in the temple ordinance of baptism for the dead where a location of a temple makes it possible. (D&C 128:13-18.) They ought to prepare themselves for service to their dead. The Aaronic Priesthood is a preparatory priesthood, and holders should prepare themselves for temple ordinances reserved for those of the Melchizedek Priesthood.

And, finally, those who bear the Aaronic Priesthood should prepare genealogical data for temple ordinances. They should do research on family lines. They should prepare family group sheets. They should work on their pedigree charts. They should "offer unto the Lord an offering in righteousness . . . a book containing the records of our dead." (D&C 128:24.)

CHAPTER EIGHT

Keys of the Ministering of Angels

When the angel visited Joseph Smith and Oliver Cowdery at Harmony, Pennsylvania, on May 15, 1829, and conferred the Aaronic Priesthood upon them, he said in part: "Upon you my fellow servants, in the name of Messiah I confer the Priesthood of Aaron, which holds the keys of the ministering of angels."

Do angels exist? What are they? What are their functions and purposes? What is their ministry? And what did the angel mean when he talked of the "keys of the ministering of angels"? Finally, and more importantly, what has all of this to do with us?

No less a personage than our Lord has called our attention to angels. When Jesus' disciples asked him to "declare unto us the parable of the tares of the field," he responded: "He that soweth the good seed is the Son of Man; the field is the world . . . and the reapers are the angels." (Matthew 13:36-39.) The Son of Man was and is real. He exists. The world was and is real. It has place and substance. As the Lord said, angels are real too. They are beings. They exist.

Jesus taught much about angels. He tells us what brings them joy. "Likewise, I say unto you, there is joy in the presence of the angels of God over one sinner that repenteth." (Luke 15:10.) In requiring us to become as little children in our faith, he reminds us that "in heaven their angels do always behold the face of my Father. . . ." (Matthew 18:10.) And in the last days he says they shall have to do with our very salvation. For, he says, he "shall send his angels . . . and they shall gather together his elect from the four winds. . . ." (Matthew 24:31.)

Clearly the Lord believes in and has to do with angels. Just as clearly, judging from his holy writ, he wants us to do the same. (Oscar W. McConkie, Jr., *Angels* [Salt Lake City: Deseret Book Co., 1975], p. 1.)

The Aaronic Priesthood has a special role to play with reference to ministrations of angels. Historically, angels have had to do with this order. Moses records the function of an angel incident to this ancient ministry: "And the Lord said unto Moses, Depart, and go up hence, thou and the people which thou hast brought up out of the land of Egypt, unto the land which I sware unto Abraham, to Isaac, and to Jacob, saying, Unto thy seed will I give it: And I will send an angel before thee." (Exodus 33:1-2.)

Following this same pattern in our day, the Lord said: "The power and authority of the lesser, or Aaronic Priesthood, is to hold the keys of the ministering of angels, and to administer in outward ordinances, the letter of the gospel, the baptism of repentance for the remission of sins, agreeable to the covenants and commandments." (D&C 107:20.)

God created the angels. "For by him were all things created, that are in heaven and that are in earth, visible and invisible ... all things were created by him, and for him." (Colossians 1:16-17.)

The angels are children of our Father in heaven. "Because angels are of the same race as man and God, it is with perfect logic that in the pure language spoken by Adam, they were designated Anglo-man." (Bruce R. McConkie, *Mormon Doctrine*, p. 37.)

Form of Angels

The spirit form and appearance are similar to the temporal form or appearance. This is true of each particular form of life. The Prophet Joseph Smith explained this principle, saying: "... that which is temporal in the likeness of that which is spiritual; the spirit of man in the likeness of his person, as also the spirit of the beast, and every other creature which God has created." (D&C 77:2). Thus in pre-earth life God's creations appeared somewhat as they appear in the flesh.

The Brother of Jared was accorded the singular privilege of seeing the Lord two millennia prior to his earthly ministry. In introducing himself the Lord said, "Behold, I am he who was prepared from the foundation of the world to redeem my people. Behold, I am Jesus Christ. ..." (Ether 3:14.) Then the Lord told his beholder, "... Seest thou that ye are created after mine own image? Yea, even all men were created in the beginning after mine own image." (Ether 3:15.) Then the Lord told him what spirits look like before they are in the flesh. Their fleshy temples are after the similitude of the spirit. "Behold, this body, which ye now behold, is the body of my spirit; and man have I created after the body of my spirit; and even as I appear unto thee to be in the spirit will I appear unto my people in the flesh." (Ether 3:16.)

Angels are in form like man, as they have appeared throughout the ages. The most universally accepted accounts of such appearances are biblical.

When Abraham entertained three angels on the plains of Mamre, it is recorded, ". . . he lift up his eyes and looked, and, lo, three men stood by him." (Genesis 18:2.) Of the two angels who visited Lot's home in Sodom, the local residents inquired, "Where are the men which came in to thee this night?" (Genesis 19:1, 5.)

Daniel described Gabriel as he came to him as being in the form of man: ". . . behold, there stood before me as the appearance of a man." (Daniel 8:15.)

All four Gospel accounts of the women at the sepulchre of the risen Lord describe "the angel of the Lord descended from heaven" (Matthew 28:2) as being in the form of a man. ". . . they saw a young man sitting on the right side, clothed in a long white garment." (Mark 16:5.) In the Gospel of John the women were pictured as seeing two angels. (John 20:12.) Luke records the same instance: "two men stood by them in shining garments." (Luke 24:4.) Although in form like men, there was a glory that attended this angel: "His countenance was like lightning, and his raiment white as snow." (Matthew 28:3.)

The most detailed description of an angel recorded was written by Joseph Smith. It is a description of the appearance of the Angel Moroni. Here is his witness:

While I was thus in the act of calling upon God, I discovered a light appearing in my room, which continued to increase until the room was lighter than at noonday, when immediately a personage appeared at my bedside, standing in the air, for his feet did not touch the floor.

He had on a loose robe of most exquisite whiteness. It was a whiteness beyond anything earthly I had ever seen; nor do I believe that any earthly thing could be made to appear so exceedingly white and brilliant. His hands were naked, and his arms also, a little above the wrist; so, also, were his feet naked, as were his legs, a little above the ankles. His head and neck were also bare. I could discover that he had no other clothing on but this robe, as it was open, so that I could see into his bosom.

Not only was his robe exceedingly white, but his whole person was glorious beyond description, and his countenance truly like lightning. The room was exceedingly light, but not so very bright as immediately around his person. When I first looked upon him, I was afraid; but the fear soon left me.

He called me by name, and said unto me that he was a messenger sent from the presence of God to me, and that his name was Moroni; that God had a work for me to do; and that my name should be had for good and evil among all nations, kindreds, and tongues, or that it should be both good and evil spoken of among all people.

After this communication, I saw the light in the room begin to gather immediately around the person of him who had been speaking to me, and it continued to do so until the room was again left dark, except just around him; when, instantly I saw, as it were, a conduit open right up into heaven, and he ascended till he entirely disappeared, and the room was left as it had been before this heavenly light had made its appearance. (Joseph Smith 2:30-33, 43.)

This vision was repeated three times, and the Prophet Joseph Smith himself wrote the firsthand account of it.

Types and Kinds of Angels

The scriptures describe several types of persons that the Lord has used as angels in varying circumstances, including the following:

1. Preexistent Spirits. In our pre-earth life John the Revelator speaks of us as angels: "Michael and his angels fought against the dragon; and the dragon fought and his angels." (Revelation 12:7.) These were the children of the Father before the earth was created. (Abraham 3:22-28.) One of these appeared to Adam and asked why he was offering sacrifices. (Moses 5:6-8.) Adam was the first man, and no activities in the nature of death or translation had taken place. Only persons assigned to this earth minister to it. (D&C 130:5.) Therefore

this angel was a preexistent spirit. These were the only persons available for use at that time.

2. Translated Beings. "And the Lord called his people Zion, because they were of one heart and one mind, and dwelt in righteousness; and there was no poor among them. . . . he built a city that was called the City of Holiness, even Zion. . . . and lo, Zion, in process of time, was taken up into heaven." (Moses 7:18-21.) This is the city of Enoch.

From the foregoing quotation we note that many people have been translated in the history of this earth. The Prophet Joseph Smith gives us more insight into this in the Inspired Version, Genesis 14:25-26.

The Prophet said of Enoch: "He is a ministering angel, to minister to those who shall be heirs of salvation, and appeared unto Jude." He further plainly says that these translated beings are "ministering angels unto many planets." (*Teachings*, p. 120.)

The Three Nephites were spoken of "as the angels of God" (3 Nephi 28:30) after they were translated and continued to minister to mortal men.

John the Revelator was translated and given to "tarry till I come." (John 21:20-25.) He ministered to Joseph Smith and Oliver Cowdery in connection with the restoration of the Melchizedek Priesthood. (D&C 7; 27:12-13.)

3. Spirits of Just Men Made Perfect. There are many persons, "an innumerable company of angels" (D&C 76:67), who are awaiting the day of their resurrection. These are "spirits of just men made perfect, they who are not resurrected, but inherit the same [heavenly] glory." (D&C 129:3.) "These are they whose names are written in heaven, where God and Christ are the judge of all. These are they who are just men made perfect. . . ." (D&C 76:68-69.)

Church leaders of spiritual maturity and sensitivity, such as President Wilford Woodruff, record many ministrations of such angels: "Joseph Smith visited me a great deal after his death, and taught me many important principles." (*The Dis-*

courses of Wilford Woodruff [Bookcraft, 1946], p. 288.)

4. Resurrected Personages. Jesus was the first person to be resurrected. Since his resurrection many persons have been resurrected, and several of these resurrected persons have come to earth as angels. (Matthew 27:52-53; Helaman 14:25.) Such angels have bodies of flesh and bones. (D&C 129.)

This type of angel has been instrumental in the restoration of the gospel in this dispensation. It was of such angels that John recorded: "And I saw another angel fly in the midst of heaven, having the everlasting gospel to preach unto them that dwell on the earth, and to every nation, and kindred, and tongue, and people." (Revelation 14:6.) He saw in vision the restoration of the gospel in these last days.

John the Baptist was such an angel. (D&C 13.) Peter and James were among this type of ministrants. (D&C 27:12-13; 128:20.)

Moroni, Michael, Gabriel, Raphael (D&C 128:20-21), Moses, Elijah, and Elias (D&C 110:11-16; 133:54-55) all came to earth as resurrected personages and played an indispensable part in the restoration in the fulness of times. They restored the keys and powers and authorities that they had obtained in their separate dispensations, thus bringing all together in one dispensation.

Moses and Elias were translated beings in their lifetimes. They ministered as such on the Mount of Transfiguration. (Matthew 17:1-4.) However, for their participation in the great drama of the dispensation of the fulness of times they "were with Christ in his resurrection." (D&C 133:55.)

It is of these angels and others like them that the revelation records: "Then shall the angels be crowned with the glory of his might, and the saints shall be filled with his glory, and receive their inheritance and be made equal with him." (D&C 88:107.) That is to say, worthy saints and angels will receive exaltation with God.

Not all angels will be exalted. Those who did not abide all of the gospel law shall not go on to godhood, but shall act as "angels of God forever and ever" and shall be "ministering servants, to minister for those who are worthy of a far more, and an exceeding, and an eternal weight of glory." (D&C 132:16-17.)

The Lord as an Angel

Our Lord is called The Angel in a blessing given by Jacob: "God, before whom my fathers Abraham and Isaac did walk, the God which fed me all my life long unto this day, The Angel which redeemed me from all evil, bless the lads." (Genesis 48:15-16.)

The Lord is not an angel in the usual sense. However, Christ is the messenger of salvation and the messenger of the covenant. (Malachi 3:1.) He is one who carries out the will of the Father. (Moses 4:2.) Thus he may perform the function of an angel and is properly called such.

It was the Lord who appeared to Moses in the burning bush: "The presence of the Lord appeared unto him, in a flame of fire in the midst of a bush." (Inspired Version, Exodus 3:2.) The King James translation interpreted the passage as "the angel of the Lord," but had him say "I am the God of thy father." (Exodus 3:2-6.) Some biblical citations thus refer to the Lord as an angel.

Righteous Mortal Men as Angels

The revelations refer to certain mortal men who act as messengers or agents of God as angels. In the Old Testament the terms "angels" and "men" were used interchangeably in talking of the persons sent by God to rescue Lot from the wicked inhabitants of Sodom. Joseph Smith's Inspired Version tells us that these "angels of God" were actually "holy men." (Inspired Version, Genesis 19:15.)

The New Testament also uses this terminology. It records the Lord as giving "unto the angel of the church of Ephesus" (Revelation 2:1) certain instructions. Thus an officer in the church was referred to as an angel.

Ministering of Angels

Angels are ministers of Christ. One of their duties is to minister to the children of men, to prepare the way for men to have faith in Christ. (Moroni 7:29-32.) Moroni says that angels have not ceased to minister:

> For behold, they are subject unto him, to minister according to the word of his command, showing themselves unto them of strong faith and a firm mind in every form of godliness.
> And the office of their ministry is to call men unto repentance, and to fulfill and to do the work of the covenants of the Father, which he hath made into the children of men, to prepare the way among the children of men, by declaring the word of Christ unto the chosen vessels of the Lord, that they may bear testimony of him. (Moroni 7:30-31.)

As angels minister to men, they "speak by the power of the Holy Ghost; wherefore, they speak the words of Christ." (2 Nephi 32:3.)

From Adam until the present day angels have ministered to men whenever men have had sufficient faith. When men are unacquainted with such ministrants it is because of unbelief. "Have angels ceased to appear unto the children of men? . . . Nay; . . . it is by faith that angels appear and minister unto men; wherefore, if these things have ceased wo be unto the children of men, for it is because of unbelief, and all is vain." (Moroni 7:36-37.)

This combination of heavenly and earthly activity is cited as a standard. If angels minister to men, then it is evidenced that they are the Lord's people and kingdom. If angels do not minister among people, it is evidenced that they are not the Lord's people.

The restoration of the gospel was foreseen as the work of ministering angels. "And I saw another angel fly in the midst of heaven, having the everlasting gospel to preach unto them that dwell on the earth, and to every nation, and kindred, and tongue, and people, Saying with a loud voice, Fear God, and give glory to him; for the hour of his judgment is come: and worship him that made heaven, and earth, and the sea, and the fountains of waters." (Revelation 14:6-7.)

It was by this means that the Book of Mormon was brought forth. "God ministered unto [Joseph Smith] by an holy angel . . . And gave him power . . . to translate the Book of Mormon." (D&C 20:6-8.)

Angels restored the Aaronic and the Melchizedek priesthoods by conferring their powers upon men.

It was because men heard the voices of angels that they were commissioned to use the keys of the kingdom in this dispensation. "Moses appeared before us, and committed unto us the keys of the gathering of Israel. . . . Elias appeared, and committed the dispensation of the gospel of Abraham. . . . Elijah . . . stood before us, . . . testifying that he [Elijah] should . . . turn the hearts of the fathers to the children, and the children to the fathers, . . . Therefore, the keys of this dispensation are committed into your hands." (D&C 110:11-16.) "The voice of Michael on the banks of the Susquehanna" (D&C 128:20) was heard by Joseph Smith. "The voice of Gabriel, and of Raphael, and of divers angels, . . . all declaring their dispensation, their rights, their keys, their honors, their majesty and glory" (D&C 128:21) were all parts of the restoration of all things.

It is by angelic ministrants that the world is called to repentance. (D&C 43:25.) It is through the ministering of angels to men in modern history that the Lord is performing his great work of restoring the gospel of Jesus Christ in principle and power.

Angels and Us

Angelic ministrations to others are vital to us. Each of us has the right to have angels minister to us. God is no respector of persons. If we comply with the requisite law, the effect of the law is put into operation. The angel Moroni need not appear to us because the Book of Mormon has already been brought forth; so also the other angels instrumental in restoring the gospel need not appear to us personally because they have already accomplished their various purposes. The Lord does not use special messengers when it is not necessary. However, the promise of angelic ministrations is not given just to persons who had part in the great restoration of things. It is a gift that all members of the priesthood should enjoy.

In speaking of the time shortly after his conversion to the Church, Wilford Woodruff reports that he baptized men but did not have the authority to confirm them. He said: "I had the administration of angels while holding the office of a priest." (*The Discourses of Wilford Woodruff* [Bookcraft, 1946], p. 298.) The illustration he uses in conjunction with this statement is illuminating. He was threatened by an apostate who intended to kill him, and his life was spared by dramatic divine intervention in his behalf. He referred to this incident as ministration of angels.

There are many specific instances in which angels have performed particular works whereby faithful people have been guarded and preserved. Isaiah writes of the angel whose presence saved Israel. (Isaiah 63:6-9.)

The administration of angels need not be as dramatic as were those of the restoring agents from on high. Angels may minister and the recipient need not know the source of his strength or joy. For example, one person may be helped while speaking from the pulpit, while another may receive guidance at a critical junction in his life. In some instances a third party has been aware of the presence of angels while the party actually concerned was apparently unaware of their presence.

One manifestation of angelic ministrations may be angels attending a person to comfort, encourage, and enlarge his joy. It was thus that Cornelius sought and enjoyed the ministration of an angel. (Acts 10:30-31.)

We have the right today to expect angels to function and perform as they have functioned and performed in times past. Those who are prepared in righteousness may claim such experiences, and if we do not enjoy them, it is because of our unbelief. The divine standard is constant. It is we who are on trial, not the angels.

Keys of the Ministering of Angels

The Aaronic Priesthood holds the keys to the ministering of angels, which means that the Aaronic Priesthood opens the door to all that we have discussed relative to the ministering of angels. Inasmuch as this is the express potential of the priesthood bearer, one is not fully enjoying his office and calling in the absence of such a wonderous experience.

What a tremendous advantage it is to hold the Aaronic Priesthood!

The Lord has ordained the lesser priesthood so that we might prepare ourselves for the high priesthood. The keys of the ministration of angels have been given to be used, and when we do not use these offered blessings, we default in our priestly prerogatives and do not enjoy the full intent of the office and callings to which we have been ordained. These proffered blessings are a means of leading us "unto the city of the living God." (Hebrews 12:22.)

David praised the Lord for this principle. "The angel of the Lord encampeth round about them that fear him, and delivereth them. O fear the Lord, ye his saints: for there is no want to them that fear him." (Psalm 34:7, 9.) He knew what he was talking about. He had experienced the angelic forces of God in his behalf. In inspired song he sang: "He hath delivered my soul in peace from the battle that was against me:

for there were many with me." (Psalm 55:18.) This is an apparent reference to the Assyrian invasion of Judah wherein the righteous troops were encouraged: "Be strong and courageous, be not afraid nor dismayed for the king of Assyria, nor for all the multitude that is with him: for there be more with us than with him: With him is an arm of flesh; but with us is the Lord our God to help us, and to fight our battles. . . ." (2 Chronicles 32:7-8.)

One trouble is that we do not know that the Lord is willing to take care of our wants, and so we do not enjoy the joint effort that we otherwise might have.

In the Old Testament we read of Elisha, a man of God who saw the angelic hosts marshaled in favor of the forces of righteousness. By intercessory prayer the prophet was able to open the eyes of the people, and they became aware of the strength of their position. They saw that there were more that were for them than there were that were against them:

Therefore sent he thither horses, and chariots, and a great host: and they came by night, and compassed the city about.

And when the servant of the man of God was risen early, and gone forth, behold, an host compassed the city both with horses and chariots. And his servant said unto him, Alas, my master! how shall we do?

And he answered, Fear not: for they that be with us are more than they that be with them.

And Elisha prayed, and said, Lord, I pray thee, open his eyes, that he may see. And the Lord opened the eyes of the young man; and he saw: and, behold, the mountain was full of horses and chariots of fire round about Elisha. (2 Kings 6:14-17.)

Since God is no respector of persons, we can safely assume that he will treat us as he treated Elisha's men. It is as important in our lives, as it was in theirs, to know that "they that be with us are more than they that be with them."

The apostle Paul talks about the Mosaic dispensation as being received "by the disposition of angels." (Acts 7:53.) This is yet another reference to the connection between the Aaronic order and angelic administrations. Apparently when God was with Moses on Sinai thousands of angels were there too. (Deuteronomy 33:2.)

As the eyes of our understanding are opened, it is hoped that we too may see. This is the reason why this order of the preparatory priesthood holds the keys to the ministering of angels.

CHAPTER NINE

Invite All to
Come Unto Christ

Apart of the specific requirements of those holding the
Aaronic Priesthood is this divine fiat: "Invite all to come unto
Christ." (D&C 20:59.) The Lord required all who have heard
the gospel to share it: "It becometh every man who hath been
warned to warn his neighbor." (D&C 88:81.) But to those of
the Aaronic Priesthood is given the special charge to invite all
into the glories of the fulness of the gospel, for priesthood
carries with it the responsibility to do missionary work.

President Spencer W. Kimball has instructed: "The question is frequently asked: Should every young man fill a mission? And the answer has been given by the Lord. It is 'yes.'
Every young man should fill a mission. . . . The answer is yes.
Every man should also pay his tithing. Every man should
observe the Sabbath. Every man should attend his meetings.

Every man should consummate his marriage in the temple. . . . yes, we would say, every able worthy man should shoulder the cross. . . ." (Regional Representatives Seminar, April 4, 1974; personal correspondence.)

Fulfilling a tour of duty as a full-time missionary is as incumbent upon a priesthood bearer as are paying tithing, keeping the Sabbath holy, and keeping the rest of the commandments. God requires it of his people.

A young missionary in the mission field came to me one day and said, "President, I want to go home."

"Why?" I asked.

He responded, "I just don't like missionary work. It is not what I expected when I accepted my call."

"I don't consider that answer responsive to my question. Why do you want to go home?"

"I told you," he replied. "I don't like missionary work; that's why I want to go home."

"Whether you like it or not doesn't have anything to do with performing your missionary obligations," I said. "Do you hold the priesthood?"

"You know I do, and I'm proud of it."

I explained, "Holding the priesthood carries with it the concomitant responsibility to do missionary service. If you like to do this type of service, that's fortunate because it means you will do what you like to do. If you don't like to do this service, it simply means that you will spend the next two years doing what you don't like to do."

When the young man understood that missionary service was not optional, he started to like it. He became an effective and happy servant of the Lord.

What Is Expected of Missionaries

"If there were no converts, the Church would shrivel and die on the vine." (Spencer W. Kimball, *op. cit.*) Missionaries are the first line of defense for the kingdom of God.

Missionary work is daily combat with sin and error, and to be successful, these troops need a very special discipline.

The first discipline of the successful missionary is to teach by the Spirit. "I the Lord ask you this question — unto what were ye ordained? To preach my gospel by the Spirit, even the Comforter which was sent forth to teach the truth. . . . And if it be by some other way it is not of God." (D&C 50:13-14, 18.) "And the Spirit shall be given unto you by the prayer of faith; and if ye receive not the Spirit ye shall not teach." (D&C 42:14.)

The Spirit is given by the prayer of faith. We must want the Spirit enough to fast and pray for it. "Behold, I have fasted and prayed many days that I might know these things of myself. And now I do know of myself that they are true; for the Lord God hath made them manifest unto me by his Holy Spirit; and this is the spirit of revelation which is in me." (Alma 5:46.) Yearning and hoping and praying are not enough. We must act. We must do what the Lord requires — keep the commandments. The Spirit will not dwell in an unclean tabernacle, for "the Lord hath said he dwelleth not in unholy temples, but in the hearts of the righteous doth he dwell." (Alma 34:36.) We must work, for "faith without works is dead." (James 2:26.)

A mission president reported this experience in general conference:

I am thankful for the Priesthood activity of the Church. I want to increase my faith in God. From the time I was a little boy, I have prayed with earnest devotion that I might have faith in God, and I remember one time, after I was a man, I had a serious problem before me — it was in the California Mission — and on my bended knees I prayed to God for strength, for wisdom, for understanding sufficient to enable me to accomplish my work, and I shall never forget how it was brought home to me that humility and righteousness are necessary in this work.

As I arose from my knees, the voice of the Spirit spoke to my spirit, for I had asked God to give me faith like unto Enoch and Elijah, because I felt that I must have that kind of faith to accomplish the purpose I was required to seek to accomplish. And the voice of the Spirit said to me: "Enoch and Elijah obtained their faith through righteousness."

Ah! there is a challenge to every man in this Church to have faith through righteousness. There is no other means of obtaining it, and we may pray until our voices fade away, but if we do not have righteousness in our daily lives, we will never have enough faith to win salvation. (*Conference Report*, October 1952, pp. 56-57.)

To get the Spirit and be worthy of acceptation by God, it is necessary to petition the Lord and to do the work.

Another discipline of a successful missionary is the attitude of success. He must *believe* that he will succeed. "All things are possible to him that believeth." (Mark 9:23.) To the missionary God has said, "The voice of warning shall be unto all people, by the mouths of my disciples, whom I have chosen in these last days. And they shall go forth and none shall stay them, for I the Lord have commanded them." (D&C 1:4-5.) When we understand that we are on the Lord's errand, we have the attitude of success.

Another discipline of a successful missionary is that of studying and learning the gospel. Gospel knowledge is a great motivator. We are under divine injunction to "teach one another the doctrine of the kingdom." (D&C 88:77.) A missionary must be familiar with the standard works of the Church. He must memorize the discussions in the standard gospel presentation plan, including all scriptures cited in the lessons. He must be familiar with and know thoroughly all tracts and pamphlets used in the work. He should think and talk about the gospel nearly all the time.

Preparation for a Mission

A person does not spring, full bloom, into a mature, productive missionary. He grows through careful cultivation. His whole life should be a preparation to invite persons to come unto Christ. Once again, the Aaronic Priesthood is the preparatory agency to assist in this noble task. It is the garden whence the flowering missionary blooms.

Before a mission call is issued, there are searching interviews to determine worthiness to serve. One of these is between the priest and his quorum president, the bishop. The candidate must be assessed as undefiled, for if he is not chaste, the call will not be made. Virtue is a vital part of the preparation for a mission.

The plan of salvation consists in overcoming the world. It is a matter of putting off the natural man and becoming a saint. (Mosiah 3:19.) As an elemental step in preparing for a mission, a priest must so participate in God's plan as to overcome the world. (John 16:33.)

Financial Preparation

The church and kingdom of God is physical as well as spiritual in nature. Members must be concerned with temporal as well as spiritual matters. Thus, preparation for complete and effective missionary service includes financial preparation.

Thrift is a virtue, and waste is accounted as a sin. (Luke 16:1-3.) Saints are under scriptural instruction to practice economy and exercise good management over their monies and properties. (D&C 59:16-20; Matthew 25:14-29.) One purpose of thrift and frugality is to amass the means of furthering the work of the kingdom.

The Church does not have a professional ministry, so in order to carry out the priesthood obligation of full-time missionary service, a person must prepare himself financially Aaronic Priesthood bearers should have savings plans set apart for future full-time missionary calls. Such funds serve two purposes: (1) to point the attention of a young man toward his future opportunity and obligation, and (2) to provide the means of so serving.

Parents and relatives have responsibilities to see that means are available for family members who are otherwise ready to respond to a mission call. Priesthood quorums are under responsibility to assist missionaries under some circumstances.

The Lord provides the bounties of the earth. We are to turn them to the use of his work. (D&C 104:11-18.)

Intellectual Preparation

Intellect has to do with the powers of the mind by which men may know, reason, and think. It is the faculty of comprehending by reason, as distinguished from the power to feel. Outside of revealed gospel truth, there is no sufficient explanation of the mind of man; through the gospel we understand that the mind rests in the eternal spirit. Man's intelligence is in his spirit and not in the mortal body. The Prophet Joseph Smith speaks of the mind or intelligence of man as being in the immortal spirit. (*Teachings*, pp. 352-53.)

With specific reference to missionaries who are sent "out to testify and warn the people," the revelation requires a course of learning. It is through the learning process "that ye may be prepared" to accomplish "the mission with which I have commissioned you." (D&C 88:80-81.)

And I give unto you a commandment that you shall teach one another the doctrine of the kingdom.

Teach ye diligently and my grace shall attend you, that you may be instructed more perfectly in theory, in principle, in doctrine, in the law of the gospel, in all things that pertain unto the kingdom of God, that are expedient for you to understand;

Of things both in heaven and in the earth, and under the earth; things which have been, things which are, things which must shortly come to pass; things which are at home, things which are abroad; the wars and the perplexities of the nations, and the judgments which are on the land; and a knowledge also of countries and of kingdoms —

That ye may be prepared in all things when I shall send you again to magnify the calling whereunto I have called you, and the mission with which I have commissioned you.

Behold, I sent you out to testify and warn the people, and it becometh every man who hath been warned to warn his neighbor. (D&C 88:77-81.)

No less a person than our Lord himself directs us to "search the scriptures; for in them ye think ye have eternal life: and they are they which testify of me." (John 5:39.) In our day he expands this instruction to include more than the scriptures: "Seek ye out of the best books words of wisdom; seek learning, even by study and also by faith." (D&C 88:118.)

The plan of salvation is a reasonable plan, a plausible explanation of where we come from, why we are here, and where we are going. Being able to present the truth in a logical way is part of the preparation for a mission. The chief apostle, Peter, counsels us to "be ready always to give an answer to every man that asketh you a reason of the hope that is in you." (1 Peter 3:15.)

Physical Preparation

It is a great privilege to have a body. We are the offspring of God (Acts 17:26, 29) clothed in mortal bodies (Moses 3:5-7). These bodies are not wholly our own to do with as we please; we have a responsibility to them. (1 Corinthians 6:19-20; 3:16-17.) True religion has to do with our temporal bodies just as it has to do with our immortal spirits.

Missionary work is just that — work! It is exacting, strength-draining endeavor that takes physical stamina. Part of the preparation for a mission is to prepare our physical body for the rigors of proselyting.

The Lord has given us revelations relative to our body's proper care. When the Aaronic order held sway he gave elaborate health codes. (Leviticus 11.) In our day, on February 27, 1833, he gave a part of his law of health, which we know as the Word of Wisdom. (D&C 89.)

The Word of Wisdom contains both positive and negative instructions. The affirmative provisions call for the wise use of meat and grain and fruit; the prohibitions direct us to refrain from the use of certain harmful things, including tobacco, alcoholic beverages, and hot drinks (tea and coffee). Compliance to the Word of Wisdom has come to show an acceptance of Christian discipline, while noncompliance signifies rebellion. It is one standard and sign that sets the Saints apart from the world.

The Word of Wisdom has particular applicability to those who hold the Aaronic Priesthood because one cannot hold office therein without adhering to it. "No official member in this Church is worthy to hold an office after having the word of wisdom properly taught him; and he, the official member, neglecting to comply with and obey it." (*Teachings*, p. 117.)

Missionaries in the field have been given exercises to tone muscles, and those who anticipate this work should do the same. Physical cleanliness and appearance are part of one's general health. These are temporal matters with spiritual overtones.

The Lord wants us to be able to "run and not be weary, and . . . walk and not faint." (D&C 89:20.)

Spiritual Preparation

It is written that Adam "became spiritually dead" (D&C 29:41) when he transgressed the law. Spiritual death is to be cast out of the presence of God.

Spiritual life is to be alive to things of righteousness and the Spirit. "We know that we have passed from death unto life, because we love the brethren. He that loveth not his brother abideth in death." (1 John 3:14.) Those who enjoy the manifestations and companionship of the Holy Ghost are spiritually alive.

The fundamental responsibility of one holding the Aaronic Priesthood is to become spiritual. The very purpose of the Aaronic Order and the "law of carnal commandments" (D&C 84:27; Hebrews 7:16) is to teach us to overcome worldliness and advance to a condition where the Spirit of the Lord can have full access to our hearts.

We all have the responsibility to develop a greater proclivity toward the things of God, and one of the greatest endowments a mortal can receive is the gift of spirituality. All men don't have the same inclination toward spiritual things. Some readily accept truth while others labor to achieve it. Of all talents to be sought after, none is greater than the talent of spirituality.

While on my first mission I received a letter from my father telling me of the wondrous working of the Spirit in his field of labor. I said to my mission president, "If the Lord wanted me to say the things I've heard my father say, He would have to speak with a loud voice." My wise leader responded, "Perhaps your father has better ears." Part of our preparation is to develop the ears to hear God's voice. "I will tell you in your mind and in your heart, by the Holy Ghost, . . . this is the spirit of revelation." (D&C 8:2-3.)

The sole perfect example of a wholly spiritual person is that of our Lord, and the simplest directive as to how to achieve this holy state was given by him: "Follow thou me." (2 Nephi 31:10.) Obedience is the basis of all righteous progression.

CHAPTER TEN

Priesthood Enlarges the Soul

Priesthood is bestowed by God for the use and benefit of man. God said to Abraham, "I will bless thee above measure, and make thy name great among all nations, and thou shalt be a blessing unto thy seed after thee, that in their hands they shall bear this ministry and Priesthood unto all nations; And I will bless them through thy name; . . . and in thee (that is, in thy Priesthood) . . . shall all the families of the earth be blessed. . . ." (Abraham 2:9-11.)

How is the world blessed through the priesthood? Through the blessings of the gospel. Since the priesthood administers the gospel ordinances, in a very real sense it administers the blessings of salvation to the world.

As the president of the Aaronic Priesthood within the ward over which he is set apart to preside, a bishop holds the keys of baptism within that jurisdiction. Since all accountable persons must be baptized to enter into the kingdom of God (John 3:3-7), the bishop thus holds the keys to salvation for all persons within his jurisdiction. The priesthood "administereth the gospel" (D&C 84:17-19), as modern scripture says.

Everything connected with the priesthood is designed to point man's attention to God, to mark his course leading to eternal life.

The Lord uses his power and authority — the priesthood — to accomplish his purposes. He revealed to Moses his grand purpose: "For behold, this is my work and my glory — to bring to pass the immortality and eternal life of man." (Moses 1:39.) The purpose of the priesthood, then, is to bring about God's work of saving mankind, the ultimate benefit to man.

Paul taught this concept, saying, "For the kingdom of God is not in word, but in power." (1 Corinthians 4:20.) Oh, how this truth needs to be understood by all peoples! It is not enough to have the Bible. It is not enough to know what God and angels say. It is not enough to know the doctrines of salvation. Standing alone, these do not bring eternal life. Men must have the word, and they must learn the doctrines of salvation; but they do not gain the kingdom of God until they possess the power of God. The gospel "is the power of God unto salvation." (Romans 1:16.) There must be power; that is, there must be priesthood. Where God's power is manifest, there is the church and kingdom of God on earth. Where his power is not found, there the church and kingdom is not. Therefore, where the priesthood is, there is the church and kingdom of God.

What are the manifestations of God's power? They are found in baptism unto the forgiveness of sins, the gift of the Holy Ghost, revelation, visions, miracles, administrations, healings, eternal marriage, and other endowments.

The gospel of Jesus Christ serves to make bad men good and good men better. We are magnified by the word and the power. Priesthood enlarges the soul and ennobles our natures. It "administereth the gospel and holdeth the key of the mysteries of the kingdom, even the key of the knowledge of God." (D&C 84:19.) And, finally, "all they who receive this priesthood receive me, saith the Lord." (D&C 84:35.)

Chosen for Service

In addressing the early converts to the true Christian faith, Peter said: "But ye are a chosen generation, a royal priesthood, an holy nation, a peculiar people; that ye should shew forth the praises of him who hath called you out of darkness into his marvellous light: Which in time past were not a people, but are now the people of God: which had not obtained mercy, but now have obtained mercy." (1 Peter 2:9-10.)

Who is the chosen generation? Peter is not talking about people living in a particular period of time. He is talking about people in all ages — the house of Israel in Old Testament times, in New Testament times, and in these latter-days. "But thou, Israel, art my servant, Jacob whom I have chosen, the seed of Abraham my friend. Thou whom I have taken from the ends of the earth, and called thee from the chief men thereof, and said unto thee, Thou art my servant; I have chosen thee, and not cast thee away." (Isaiah 41:8-9.) Please note the terminology of the Lord: these persons were *chosen* to be servants.

Whenever the Lord has a people on the earth, he offers to make them a people composed of kings and priests. That is, he anticipates a whole church consisting of persons who serve as their own ministers. He envisions every man standing as a king in his own right, reigning over his own family-kingdom. The priesthood that makes a man a king and a priest is thus a royal priesthood.

God's offer to ancient Israel was made in these words: "If ye will obey my voice indeed, and keep my covenant, then ye shall be a peculiar treasure unto me above all people: for all the earth is mine: And ye shall be unto me a kingdom of priests, and an holy nation." (Exodus 19:5-6.) Peter told the saints in the Meridian of Time that they have the same promise. It is later recorded that some of these saints did obtain this promise and, in due course of time, will reign with Christ at his Second Coming. (Revelation 1:6; 5:10; 20:4.)

The same blessings are available to Latter-day Saints. The preparatory priesthood, the Order of Aaron, is the beginning of these blessings.

It pleases God when his servants serve their fellowmen. Indeed, his priesthood bearers are chosen to so serve. The inspired wisdom of King Benjamin is recorded in his great farewell address: "When ye are in the service of your fellow beings ye are only in the service of your God." (Mosiah 2:17.) The apostle Paul states how he serves the Lord: "Christ sent me . . . to preach the gospel." (1 Corinthians 1:17.) Aaronic Priesthood holders are directed to serve in like manner (D&C 20:46) in this day. For what are we chosen? Service.

The people of God are those who join his church. They are adopted into his family and set apart from the world. They become part of the kingdom of Israel, in which, in our day, they enjoy an almost universal priesthood concept.

I can think of no better way to assure fulfillment in one's life than to attach oneself to the purposes of God and serve therein until fruition is had. As God's purposes are accomplished, man's are magnified.

Love and Service

The highest manifestation of man's love is found in his devotion to God. "Hear, O Israel: The Lord our God is one Lord: And thou shalt love the Lord thy God with all thine heart, and with all thy soul, and with all thy might." (Deuteronomy 6:4-5.) Moses said this was the "commandments, the statute and the judgments" that the Lord directed him to teach to Israel. When Jesus was asked which was the great commandment of the law, he answered, "Thou shalt love the Lord thy God with all thy heart, and with all thy soul, and with all thy mind. This is the first and great commandment." (Matthew 22:37-38.) And indeed it is. All good centers in God. Man's greatest good is to love God.

The Lord continued, "And the second is like unto it, thou shalt love thy neighbour as thyself." (Matthew 22:39.)

So basic to true religion is love of God and love of neighbor that the Lord says that all else is based on this. "On these two commandments," he says, "hang all the law and the prophets." (Matthew 22:40.)

These two commandments are bound together because the love of God is found only in those who love their brothers and sisters. "If a man say, I love God, and hateth his brother, he is a liar: for he that loveth not his brethren whom he hath seen, how can he love God whom he hath not seen? And this commandment we have from him, That he who loveth God love his brother also." (1 John 4:20-21.)

Service in God's purposes means dedication of oneself to righteousness and keeping the commandments. As always, the sole perfect Exemplar said and did it best: "I am among you as he that serveth." (Luke 22:27.)

Service is the child of love. It is through service that love is manifest. If love is the precept, then service is the example. Again, Jesus said, "If thou lovest me thou shalt serve me and keep all of my commandments." (D&C 42:29.) This puts the lie to those who would feign to be Christians, professing love to all of mankind in general, but who do not like their neighbors.

What doth it profit, my brethren, though a man say he hath faith, and have not works? can faith save him?

If a brother or sister be naked, and destitute of daily food,

And one of you say unto them, Depart in peace, be ye warmed and filled; notwithstanding ye give them not those things which are needful to the body; what doth it profit?

Even so faith, if it hath not works, is dead, being alone.

Yea, a man may say, Thou hast faith, and I have works: shew me thy faith without thy works, and I will shew thee my faith by my works.

Thou believest that there is one God; thou doest well: the devils also believe, and tremble.

But wilt thou know, O vain man, that faith without works is dead?

Was not Abraham our father justified by works, when he had offered Isaac his son upon the altar?

Seest thou how faith wrought with his works, and by works was faith made perfect?

And the scripture was fulfilled which saith, Abraham believed God, and it was imputed unto him for righteousness: and he was called the Friend of God.

Ye see then how that by works a man is justified, and not by faith only." (James 2:14-24.)

In King Benjamin's farewell sermon he told the listeners this fundamental truth: "And behold, I tell you these things that ye may learn wisdom; that ye may learn that when ye are in the service of your fellow beings ye are only in the service of your God. Behold, ye have called me your king; and if I, whom ye call your king, do labor to serve you, then ought not ye to labor to serve one another?" (Mosiah 2:17-18.)

The priesthood-endowed servants of God are to be known by their love and service one to another. "By this shall all men know that ye are my disciples, if ye have love one to another." (John 13:35.) One of the privileges of holding the priesthood is that it opens new vistas for service. We should thank our Heavenly Father each day for our opportunities to serve.

On the other hand, where there is no love and no service, there is iniquity: "And because iniquity shall abound, the love of many shall wax cold." (Matthew 24:12.)

Perfect love is an attribute of Deity. Thus the early apostle John said, "God is love." (1 John 4:8.) The priesthood prepares us to "be partakers of the divine nature" (2 Peter 1:4) by inculcating love into our lives.

As love grows in man, so man grows heavenward, for love is one of the gifts of the Spirit, for "the fruit of the Spirit is love. . . ."(Galatians 5:22.) Love expands man. Priesthood is God's service calling. It is a manifestation of his love.

Keep the Commandments and Ordinances

The prophets in all ages have condemned the empty formality, the useless perfunctory performances of rites and ceremonies. In the midst of the Mosaic dispensation, with its multitudes of proper performances and ordinances, the prophet Micah declared: "Will the Lord be pleased with thousands of rams or with ten thousands of rivers of oil? . . . He hath shewed thee, O man, what is good; and what doth the Lord require of thee, but to do justly, and to love mercy, and to walk humbly with thy God?" (Micah 6:7-8.)

Uninspired students have mistakenly said that the priesthood-officiated sacrificial system had no place with the prophets and that it was abandoned by them. Nothing could be further from the truth. The sacrificial system, with its priesthood performances, was divinely appointed. (Moses 5:6-8.) It was to be continued and fulfilled in Jesus Christ. One of the last acts of our Lord was to celebrate the Passover.

What Micah and all the prophets, ancient and modern, condemn is the empty, meaningless performance of ordinances: man's doing something merely to meet his religious obligation, and his ignoring the fact that what gave the performance of the rites true significance was the sincere spiritual attitude of the offerer, his authority so to do, and, finally, acceptation by God.

Micah would take the same position today — as, indeed, the modern prophets have done — regarding acts that are devoid of meaning because they are performed without authority and because the heart is unrenewed and away from God. Such censure does not apply to the true worship and

Christian rites of the kingdom of God today. The prophets upbraid spiritually decadent people for observing ordinances; they do not charge legal administrators with folly for performing righteously.

In order to be a partaker of the divine nature, man must strive to be obedient and to develop the attributes of Godliness that are inherent in him. Joseph Smith said: "If you wish to go where God is, you must be like God, or possess the principles which God possesses, for if we are not drawing towards God in principle, we are going from Him and drawing towards the devil." (*Teachings*, p. 216.) The Aaronic Priesthood is a God-ordained and God-instituted order to assist man to put on the divine nature.

In speaking of the fulness of the priesthood, Joseph Smith said: "If a man gets a fulness of the priesthood of God he has to get it in the same way that Jesus Christ obtained it, and that was by keeping all the commandments and obeying all the ordinances of the house of the Lord." (*Teachings*, p. 308.) "The question is frequently asked, 'Can we not be saved without going through with all those ordinances?' I would answer, No, not the fulness of salvation. Jesus said, There are many mansions in my Father's house, and I will go and prepare a place for you. *House* here named should have been translated kingdom; and any person who is exalted to the highest mansion has to abide a celestial law, and the whole law too." (*Teachings*, p. 331.)

This principle of the preparatory order of things was stated by a modern prophet, President Harold B. Lee, in these practical terms: "The most important of all the commandments of God is that one that you're having the most difficulty keeping today. If it's one of dishonesty, if it's one of unchastity, if it's one of falsifying, not telling the truth, today is the day for you to work on that until you've been able to conquer that weakness. Then you start on the next one that's most difficult for you to keep." (*Church News*, May 5, 1973, p. 3.) It is thus that we progress, line upon line and precept upon precept, as we learn to abide by the commandments and make the ordinances a real and meaningful part of our lives.

Obedience is the first law of heaven, the means whereby all righteousness is accomplished. It is the basis of all righteous progression. In terms of the plan of salvation, to obey is to follow the guidance of God and to execute his commands. It is to be ruled by his law. Through obedience, meaning and application of the gospel are had in our lives. It is thus a primary principle in heaven and earth.

Man's love of God is measured by his obedience. "If ye love me, keep my commandments." (John 14:15.) It is not form, but principle and service that are the measure of a man. When Saul chose to disobey counsel and to sacrifice cattle according to the religious form of his day, the ancient prophet Samuel rebuked him, saying, "Hath the Lord as great delight in burnt offerings and sacrifices, as in obeying the voice of the Lord? Behold, to obey is better than sacrifice, and to hearken than the fat of rams. For rebellion is as the sin of witchcraft, and stubbornness is as iniquity and idolatry." (1 Samuel 15:22-23.)

The very purpose of this earth life is to provide for a mortal probationary period, a testing ground, for the spirit children of our Father in heaven. "We will prove them herewith," says the divine decree, "to see if they will do all things whatsoever the Lord their God shall command them." (Abraham 3:25.) The Lord created men, placed them on the earth, "and gave unto them commandments that they should love and serve him." (D&C 20:19.) The whole system of creation and existence is bound up in the eternal principle of obedience to law.

All men are directed by divine decree to believe the gospel, to repent of their sins, to be baptized by immersion for the remission of their sins, and to endure to the end by obedience to the laws and ordinances of the gospel. It is only in this way that we obtain a hope for salvation in the kingdom of God. (2 Nephi 31; 3 Nephi 27:13-22.) Through priesthood-administered baptism, man may make the solemn covenant to serve God and keep his commandments (Mosiah 18:7-10); and this baptismal covenant may be renewed with each partaking of the priesthood-administered sacrament (D&C 20:77-79).

Priesthood-administered rites and ordinances are more than outward forms of inward graces. They are part of the warp and woof of the fabric of salvation. There is no obedience unto God's commands without them.

All That God Hath

The end of all of our belief, of all of our performances, of all of our service, of all of our doings, of all of our hope is eternal life. The word *eternal*, used in this connection in the scriptures, is not an adjective qualifying the noun *life*. It is a part of the noun. It is one of the scriptural names given to God. (Moses 1:3; 7:35; D&C 19:11.) It describes the type and kind of life that he lives: "... eternal life ... is the greatest of all the gifts of God." (D&C 14:7.) Those who gain eternal life enjoy exaltation. They are joint heirs with Christ. They are the Sons of God.

The achievement of all of this is priesthood-centered. In our day it is written:

For whoso is faithful unto the obtaining these two priesthoods of which I have spoken, and the magnifying their calling, are sanctified by the Spirit unto the renewing of their bodies.

And they become the sons of Moses and of Aaron and the seed of Abraham, and the church and kingdom, and the elect of God.

And also all they who receive this priesthood receive me, saith the Lord;

For he that receiveth my servants receiveth me;

And he that receiveth me receiveth my Father;

And he that receiveth my Father receiveth my Father's kingdom; therefore all that my Father hath shall be given unto him. (D&C 84:33-38.)

All that God hath has been promised to his children, conditioned upon their magnifying their priestly callings. God is a superlative personage, exalted, perfect in all the attributes of his nature. He is perfect in knowledge, in faith, in power. He is perfect in justice, in judgment, and in mercy. He is the Lord God omnipotent, the sole perfect manifestation of love. (Joseph Smith, *Lectures on Faith*, pp. 45-51.)

Becoming like God is a process, not an event. The Prophet Joseph Smith said: "When you climb up a ladder, you must begin at the bottom, and ascend step by step, until you arrive at the top; and so it is with the principles of the Gospel — you must begin with the first, and go on until you learn all the principles of exaltation. But it will be a great while after you have passed through the veil before you will have learned them. It is not all to be comprehended in this world; it will be a great work to learn our salvation and exaltation even beyond the grave." (*Teachings*, p. 348.)

The perfectability of man has always been the nerve center of our Lord's gospel. "Be ye therefore perfect," he said, "even as your Father which is in heaven is perfect." (Matthew 5:48.)

In his first general epistle John explains the literalness of this doctrine: "Beloved, now are we the sons of God, and it doth not yet appear what we shall be: but we know that, when he shall appear, we shall be like him; for we shall see him as he is. And every man that hath this hope in him purifieth himself, even as he is pure." (1 John 3:2-3.)

The apostle Paul shocked the traditional religionists when he discussed the Holy Ghost-taught doctrine of the perfectability of man: "Let this mind be in you, which was also in Christ Jesus: Who, being in the form of God, thought it not robbery to be equal with God. . . . Wherefore God also hath highly exalted him. . . ." (Philippians 2:5-9.)

Paul tells us that Jesus was equal with God, and John tells us that when Jesus comes a second time in his perfection and glory, we may be like him. This is all according to the doctrine of Jesus. In this last dispensation, President Lorenzo Snow penned the following response to these New Testament citations:

Dear Brother:

Hast thou not been unwisely bold,
Man's destiny to thus unfold?
To raise, promote such high desire,
Such vast ambition thus inspire?

Still, 'tis no phantom that we trace
Man's ultimatum in life's race;
This royal path has long been trod
By righteous men, each now a God:

As Abra'm, Isaac, Jacob, too,
First babes, then men — to gods they grew.
As man now is, our God once was;
As now God is, so man may be, —
Which doth unfold man's destiny

For John declares: When Christ we see
Like unto him we'll truly be.
And he who has this hope within,
Will purify himself from sin. . . .

The boy, like to his father grown,
Has but attained unto his own;
To grow to sire from state of son,
Is not 'gainst Nature's course to run.

A son of God, like God to be,
Would not be robbing Deity;
And he who has this hope within,
Will purify himself from sin.

You're right, St. John, supremely right;
Whoe'er essays to climb this height,
Will cleanse himself of sin entire —
Or else 'twere needless to aspire.

The great prophet of the dispensation of the fulness of times, Joseph Smith, said it best:

Here, then, is eternal life — to know the only wise and true God; and you have got to learn how to be Gods yourselves, and to be kings and priests to God, the same as all Gods have done before you, namely, by going from one small degree to another, and from a small capacity to a great one; from grace to grace, from exaltation to exaltation, until you attain to the resurrection of the dead, and are able to dwell in everlasting burnings, and to sit in glory, as do those who sit enthroned in everlasting power. And I want you to know that God, in the last days, while certain individuals are proclaiming his name, is not trifling with you or me. (*Teachings*, pp. 346-47.)

Bibliography

Books

A Royal Priesthood, 1975-1976. A Personal Study Guide for Melchizedek Priesthood Quorums of The Church of Jesus Christ of Latter-day Saints. Salt Lake City: Corporation of the President of The Church of Jesus Christ of Latter-day Saints, 1975.

Bible. King James Version.

Bible. Inspired Version.

Book of Mormon.

Clark, J. Reuben, Jr. *On the Way to Immortality and Eternal Life.* Salt Lake City: Deseret Book Co., 1954.

Cowley, Matthew. *Matthew Cowley Speaks.* Salt Lake City: Deseret Book Co., 1954.

Doctrine and Covenants.

Gaster, Theodore H. *The Dead Sea Scriptures.* New York: Doubleday, 1957.

General Handbook of Instructions, No. 21. Salt Lake City: Corporation of the President of The Church of Jesus Christ of Latter-day Saints, 1976.

Journal of Discourses.

Journal History. Church Historian's Office.

McConkie, Bruce R. *Doctrinal New Testament Commentary.* 3 vols. Salt Lake City: Bookcraft, 1965, 1971, 1973.

_____. *Mormon Doctrine.* 2nd ed. Salt Lake City: Bookcraft, 1966.

McConkie, Oscar W., Jr. *Angels.* Salt Lake City: Deseret Book Co., 1975.

_____. *Kingdom of God.* Salt Lake City: Corporation of the Presiding Bishop of The Church of Jesus Christ of Latter-day Saints, 1962.

_____. *God and Man.* Salt Lake City: Corporation of the Presiding Bishop of The Church of Jesus Christ of Latter-day Saints, 1963.

_____. *The Priest in the Aaronic Priesthood.* Salt Lake City: Corporation of the Presiding Bishop of The Church of Jesus Christ of Latter-day Saints, 1964.

Melchizedek Priesthood Handbook. Salt Lake City: Corporation of the First Presidency of The Church of Jesus Christ of Latter-day Saints.

Melchizedek Priesthood Quorum Study Guide, 1975-1976: A Royal Priesthood. Salt Lake City: Corporation of the President of The Church of Jesus Christ of Latter-day Saints, 1975.

Palmer, Lee A. *Aaronic Priesthood Through the Ages*. Salt Lake City: Deseret Book Co., 1964.

Robinson, O. Preston. *The Dead Sea Scrolls and Original Christianity*. Salt Lake City: Deseret Book Co., 1958.

Smith, Joseph. *History of the Church*. 7 vols., plus index. Salt Lake City: Deseret Book Co., 1951.

——————————. *Lectures on Faith*. Salt Lake City: Deseret Sunday School Union, 1913.

——————————. *Teachings of the Prophet Joseph Smith*. Compiled by Joseph Fielding Smith. Salt Lake City: Deseret Book Co., 1976.

Smith, Joseph F. *Gospel Doctrine*. Compiled by Joseph Fielding Smith. Salt Lake City: Deseret Book Co., 1970.

Smith, Joseph Fielding. *Doctrines of Salvation*. 3 vols. Compiled by Bruce R. McConkie. Salt Lake City: Bookcraft, 1954, 1955, 1956.

——————————. *Essentials in Church History*. Salt Lake City: Deseret Book Co., 1974.

Strong, James. *The Exhaustive Concordance of the Bible*. New York: Abingdon Press, 1967.

Talmage, James E. *Articles of Faith*. Salt Lake City: Deseret Book Co., 1966.

Taylor, John. *Items on Priesthood*. Salt Lake City: Deseret News Co., 1882.

Woodruff, Wilford. *The Discourses of Wilford Woodruff*. Compiled by G. Homer Durham. Salt Lake City: Bookcraft, 1946.

Young, Brigham. *Discourses of Brigham Young*. Compiled by John A. Widtsoe. Salt Lake City: Deseret Book Co., 1973.

Periodicals

Conference Report. Proceedings of the annual and semiannual general conferences of The Church of Jesus Christ of Latter-day Saints.

Church Section, Deseret News.

Messenger and Advocate, 1834.

Miscellaneous

Correspondence, letter to stake and mission presidents from the First Presidency, January 25, 1972.

Correspondence, letters to bishops from the First Presidency, 1969.

Correspondence to author from President Spencer W. Kimball, including sermon delivered to Regional Representatives of the Council of the Twelve on April 4, 1974.

Kimball, Spencer W. Address at MIA June Conference, June 1974.

Lee, Harold B. *Conference Report*, October 1972.

McConkie, Oscar W. *Conference Report*, October 1952.

Notes of Andrew Jenson, Church Historical Department.

Index

Aaron: chosen for priesthood, 19; life of, 20; death of, 21; call of, 26

Aaronic Priesthood: definition of, 4-5, 21; keys held by, 22; duties of, 22-23, 105-6; establishment of, 28; is Priesthood of Elias, 31; purpose of, 35-36; restoration of, 41-44; duration of, 63-64, 77. *See also* Priesthood

Adam given priesthood, 15

Age of ancient priesthood bearers, 27-28

Angels: reality of, 91-93; form of, 93; appearances of, 94-95; types of, 95-98; mortal men as, 98-99; duties of, 99; ministrations of, 100-2; provide protective care, 102-4. *See also* Ministering of angels

Authority: of man on earth, 2; expansion of, among members of Israel, 25

Baptism: Aaronic Priesthood holds keys of, 22; is duty of priest, 56; as part of preparatory gospel, 71; symbolism of, 72; is part of everlasting covenant, 72; characteristics of, 72-73; is initiatory ordinance, 73; is prerequisite to salvation, 73; of the Spirit, 74; means immersion, 74; proper form of, 74; purposes of, 74-75

Bishop: issues priesthood calls, 49-50; office of, 58-59; qualifications of, 59; as president of priests quorum, 61

Blind baby healed, 10

Boys, Aaronic Priesthood given to, 49

Called of God, 2, 26

Certificate of Ordination, 50

Children to be taught, 81-82

Christ. *See* Jesus Christ

Church, definition of, 54

Covenant taken at baptism, 75-76

Cowdery, Oliver, quotation from, 42-44

Cowley, Matthew, quotation from, 10-11

Deacon: qualifications for office of, 35; responsibilities of, 51-52

Dead man made whole, 10-11

Elder who had hiccups, 12-13

Elders: duties of, 38-39; prospective, 39-40

Eternal life, 79, 124-27

Evolution of God, theory of, 16

Exhort, 82-83

Expound, 82

Faith: of ancient priesthood
bearers, 11-12; brings
ministrations of angels, 99;
Spirit given by, 107

Genealogy as an offering in
righteousness, 86-87
God: power of, 1; men called by,
2; called "Righteousness," 6;
Church administered by
power of, 13-14; theory of
evolution of, 16; scriptural
accounts of, 16-17; Aaron
called by, 26; all to become
like, 125
Gospel: all to hear, 87;
priesthood is to share, 105-6
Gospel of repentance: Aaronic
Priesthood holds keys of, 22;
is preparatory gospel, 68-69.
See also Preparatory gospel;
Repentance
Grace of God, 2

Hiccups, elder who had, 12-13
Holy Ghost in teaching, 81
Home teachers: teachers as, 54;
priests as, 57; obligation of
priesthood bearers to be, 83

Israelites received Law of
Moses, 17-19

Jesus Christ: man may share
authority of, 2; called to
priesthood, 3; called "Son of
Righteousness," 6; ended
Mosaic dispensation, 29;
ended offering of sacrifices,
46; religious ordinances center
in, 71-72; as an angel, 98
John the Baptist, 30, 41-44

Keys held by Aaronic
Priesthood, 22
Kimball, Spencer W., speaks
with reporter, 13; quotations
from, 62-63, 105-6

Lame man healed by Peter, 9
Law of Moses, 17-19
Lee, Harold B., quotations from,
63, 122
Lesser priesthood, 21. *See also*
Aaronic Priesthood
Levites: to look after the
tabernacle, 25; under
direction of Aaronic
Priesthood, 27; functions of,
comparable to teachers and
deacons, 29
Levitical ordinances to be
performed in this dispensation,
45-47, 78-79
Levitical Priesthood, 23, 30. *See
also* Aaronic Priesthood
Love, 118-19, 120-21

Man: authority of, on earth, 2;
perfectability of, 125-27
Melchizedek Priesthood:
institution of, 4; is to preside,
28; was taken from Israel, 29;
Church operated by, 36. *See
also* Priesthood
Ministering of angels: Aaronic
Priesthood holds keys of, 22,
102-4; work of, 100-2. *See also*
Angels
Missionaries: all young men
should be, 105-6; disciplines
of, 106-8; financial
preparation of, 109-10;
intellectual preparation of,
110-11; physical preparation

of, 111-12; spiritual preparation of, 112-13

Moroni, appearance of, 94-95

Moses: called to priesthood, 16-17; received Ten Commandments, 17; standard raised by, 24; established Aaronic Priesthood, 28; taken from Israel, 29

Obedience, 123-24

Oblations, 78

Offering: welfare as, 86; genealogy as, 86-87

Offerings: making, is worshiping, 78-79; types of, 78

Offices: duties of priesthood, 37-38; in Aaronic Priesthood, 47-48; of priesthood in biblical times, 48-49

Omnipotent, 1-2

Ordinances: performed by ancient priesthood bearers, 23; necessary for salvation, 122

Ordination, 3, 50

Peter, 2-3, 9

Power of God, 1; Church administered by, 13-14

Preach: duty of priest, 56; a priesthood calling, 80

Preexistent spirits, 95-96

Preparatory gospel, 71. See also Gospel of repentance; Repentance

Preparatory priesthood, 22, 31. See also Aaronic Priesthood

Presiding Bishop of the Church, 60-61

Priest: Aaron was, 26; institution of office of, 55; duties of, 55-57

Priesthood: those called to, 3; name of, 4; definition of, 4; is eternal, 5, 8-9; functions of, 6; power of, 7-8; power of, for all, 12; history of, 15; in Israel was hereditary, 30; preparatory, 36; purpose of, 116; a royal, 117-18. See also Aaronic Priesthood; Melchizedek Priesthood

Priesthood bearers: good works of, 9-12; faith of, 11-12; qualifications of, 49-50

Priesthood of Elias, 31

Priesthood offices: duties of, 37-38; in Aaronic Priesthood, 47-48; in biblical times, 48-49

Prospective elders, 39-40

Quorums: organization of, 61; as service units, 62; emphasis on strengthening, 62-63

Repentance: in process of salvation, 65-66; process of, 66-68; obligation to teach others, 68. See also Gospel of repentance

Reporter who spoke with President Kimball, 13

Restoration of all things, 44-45

Resurrected personages, 97-98

Righteousness: attainment of, 5; one of God's names, 6

Sacrificial offerings: directed by Aaronic Priesthood, 29; to be performed in this dispensation, 45-47; symbolism of, 72; divinely appointed, 121-22

Sacrament administration, 56-57

Salvation: repentance essential to, 65-66; baptism prerequisite to, 73; for the dead, 87-89

Scriptural accounts: of priesthood bearers, 15; of God, 16-17

Serpent raised by Moses, 24

Service, 119-20

Smith, Joseph, quotations from 5, 41-42, 94-95, 122, 125, 127

Smoot, Reed, 32-33

Snow, Lorenzo, poem by, 125-26

Sons of God, 3

Sons of Levi, 45

Standard raised by Moses, 24

Teach: priesthood to, 6, 80-82; by the Spirit, 107-8

Teacher, responsibilities of, 53-55

Ten Commandments, 17-19

Translated beings, 96

Tribe of Levi, 25

Types of things to come, 24

Welfare, 84-85

Works of priesthood holders, 9-12

Young woman who was descendant of Levi, 31-32